A PATH OF MASTERY

Lessons on Wing Chun and Life
from Sifu Francis Fong

JIM BRAULT

Also by Jim Brault:
Lessons from the Masters: Seven Keys to Peak Performance and Inner Peace
The Winning Mind Set with co-author Kevin Seaman

The information in this book is meant to supplement, not replace, proper martial arts training. Like any activity involving speed, balance and physical contact, the practice of martial arts poses some inherent risk. The authors and publisher advise readers to take full responsibility for their safety and know their limits. Before undertaking any activity described in this book, you are advised to consult with your medical doctor, and do not take risks beyond your level of experience, aptitude, training, and comfort level.

Printed in the United States of America.

Center Line Press
249 Totem Trail
Suite 30
Rochester, NY 14617

To order additional copies of *A Path of Mastery* or to find out more about our other products and services visit: www.APathOfMastery.com

Facebook: www.facebook.com/wingchunconcepts

Editor: Abbie Saunders
First Edition
ISBN 978-0-9663482-9-3

Cover Illustration: Kevin Lee

Front and back cover design: Kevin Lee and Anna Fasolyak

Book layout and design: Anna Fasolyak

To my wife, Jessie,
who lets me train as much as I want.

CONTENTS

FOREWORD

Sifu Francis Fong is without a doubt one of the most talented and multi-dimensional martial artists teaching today.

I have known Sifu Francis for over 35 years. He is constantly researching and growing in skill and knowledge. His creativity and ability to adapt his teaching to suit the needs of his students is a rare gift.

His accomplishments and achievements are many, and I stand in awe of his martial art and healing skills. But equally, or perhaps more importantly, Sifu Francis Fong is a great human being. His humility, kindness and loyalty to his students, friends and all who have a genuine interest in the arts is boundless. I consider myself very lucky to be his friend.

Dan Inosanto
Founder / Head Instructor
Inosanto Academy of Martial Arts
Marina Del Rey, California, USA
http://www.inosanto.com/

Sifu Francis Fong and Guro Dan Inosanto

WHEN THE STUDENT IS READY

Relax. Take your time.

It's like he's in my corner instead of my head. I hear his coaching as plain as day. Cantonese intonation flavors his delivery; his words are uttered in a combination of staccato bursts and elongated syllables. Musical, on the cusp of hypnotic.

I exhale, allowing my shoulders drop. I sink my body down. Sensation guides my movements.

Are you sinking? Are you sure?

I picture the raised eyebrows and contagious grin that come right before he pushes me over to show I wasn't as rooted as I thought.

Then the deep belly laugh.

I smile and laugh too. Then I really sink.

Listen. Are you really listening?

It's not only when I'm training. I'll often hear his voice when I'm with someone and my mind is drifting to my to-do list, a pressing problem, or extraneous circumstance. I remind myself to be present.

There's an old saying: when the student is ready, the teacher will appear. On a muggy summer day in 1991, my teacher appeared. Most who meet him quickly realize that he does not simply teach martial arts. Rather, he teaches through martial arts masterfully guided lessons of far greater worth. Like finding gold amongst ordinary river stones, his students discover valuable lessons on perseverance, focus, patience, sensitivity and compassion. While teaching students to harness the staggering power of their body and mind, he shows them the even greater power of love.

Primarily his course of study was instruction in a lethal street survival system — Wing Chun Kung Fu. Interwoven throughout was something I longed for, but hadn't expected, especially coming from a person who fought in the streets of Hong Kong and New York and who trains Fort Benning Army Rangers and SWAT Teams to take care of business.

It was a series of principles for a way to live that would take years to learn, decades to fully grasp, and a lifetime to master.

An art is different than a physical workout. Art is never done.
When will you be done? When you are in your coffin; then you'll be done.
That's why not many people really want to learn the art.
Mastering an art is about mastering yourself.

It was a path of mastery.

A path richly populated with lessons.

Lessons on how to live more honestly and openly, how to honor the greatness in others and ourselves, and how to be patient with our weaknesses.

Lessons on how to be in harmony with nature's song, a melody that is easy to perceive but even easier to overlook.

Lessons on acceptance, on the importance of remaining humble, and of the importance of giving generously with no expectation of anything in return.

Lessons on how to live a life based on your true nature and priorities, the criticality of finding your own path, how to harness the incredible power of your mind and body, stressing all the while that real power comes from your heart.

You want to be powerful? The real power comes from love.

At times, his teaching was delivered with explosive and forceful impact, knowing that the only way for me to understand was through unmediated experience.

At times, it came through relentless repetition, knowing that until I could stop thinking and analyzing, I would never respond naturally.

At times, it came through a nod or word of encouragement, the timing of which boosted my confidence and fueled my desire to persevere.

At times, it came through penetrating observations: always accurate and volunteered with complete clarity.

At times, it came through honest and heartfelt conversation lasting late into the night.

If I can train your body, I can open your mind.
If I can open your mind, I can open your heart.
Everybody wants results right away.
But until you work on your heart and soul, it is nothing.
It's only surface.

This man, this teacher, is Francis Fong, but everyone calls him Sifu.

Sifu means both father and teacher.
You have to love your student like you would your own son or daughter.

From the beginning of my training with Sifu, I took copious notes. At first they consisted mostly of drawings and points about techniques and training approaches for Wing Chun. But over time, I began capturing principles that expanded beyond specific techniques — lessons which could be applied beyond martial arts to both personal and professional realms.

Use your training to improve your life.

Here, I share my stories and experiences with you as context for the lessons. You won't learn from my shining examples of consistently applying his wisdom; more often than not I have struggled in my attempts to implement Sifu's sage advice.

For a time, I stopped my martial arts training altogether, substituting it with workouts that did wonders for my physique, but little else. For longer than I care to admit, I wasn't ready to work on my heart and spirit and because of that my results were, as he predicted, only on the surface. Even though I had achieved much in many areas of my life, my accomplishments rang hollow.

Accomplishments are good.
But if you aren't at peace with yourself,
what does it really matter?

I hadn't come close to mastering either the art or myself.

At one point, though, I finally grasped the value of the path he first revealed to me on that summer day in 1991. Little by little, over time, I began to apply these lessons more consistently to both my martial arts practice and to my life. With that practice and application, I experienced progress and a sense of inner peace in both realms.

With practice and application, you will too.

Through this book, it is my hope that you become familiar with these ideas, embodying what makes sense for you in your own practice and life. While they are often simple, enormous depth lies beneath the surface. Take your time with each lesson, especially those that seem to speak to you more vibrantly. In Part 1 — The Lessons, I share each lesson as it was taught to me. In Part 2 —The Lessons Revisited, I return to the lessons and offer you further ways to embody them in your art and life.

The full essence of a person can never be fully captured in the pages of a book, much more so for a teacher and martial artist as multifaceted and gifted as Sifu Francis Fong. Nevertheless, I trust that the pages that follow will provide you with a solid foundation from which to build a strong Wing Chun practice, and perhaps more importantly a more successful and happier life. Although we may all be on different paths, I believe we are all striving for the same destination.

Jim Brault
Rochester, NY USA / Cambridge UK / August 2016

Yao Ying Yao Yi Gi Si Ga
Mo Fat Mo Sum Fong Wy Jun

Forms and preconceptions create a world of illusion.
Release the methods, respond naturally and spontaneously.
This is the only way to touch genuine reality.

PART ONE: THE LESSONS

LESSON I
THE ONLY REAL FIGHT

Why bother spending years and years training in martial arts?
The answer is that even though you may never get into a fight,
you are always fighting yourself.
That's the only real fight.
Self-defense is good. Being healthy is good, too.
But if you aren't at peace with yourself, what does it really matter?
Use your training to help your life.

"Take a right up there," Matt said, pointing to a black and white sign 100 yards in the distance. I navigated the turn and followed a two-lane road overlooking the 40 mile length of Cayuga Lake, one of the seven Finger Lakes in upstate New York's wine region. The rolling hills, sandy soil and temperate climate were ideal for growing grapes. The shimmering mirage from the heat rising off the pavement ahead, however, made me wonder how the year's crop would fare with the way the summer of 1991 had been shaping up. It was only mid-June, but by noon the temperature was expected to climb to over 90 degrees, which, with the humidity, felt even hotter. Sweat trickled down my chest. I turned the fan to full blast. It had all the cooling effect of a blow dryer.

When I bought my car a year earlier I didn't want to waste money on air conditioning. Actually, I didn't want to waste money on a car at all, which is why I bought a Geo Metro. My wife, Jessie, couldn't believe what I had done when I pulled into the driveway.

"There are five people in this family, but you bought a car with four seat belts, two doors, no air conditioning, and an AM radio," she said, framed more as a statement than a question.

I don't remember my reply, but that was the last time I bought a car without her.

In my defense, it wasn't our only car. We also had a minivan. Besides, I think part of what influenced my purchase was genetic. Growing up I was the second of five kids, and until I was 17, we only had one car — a brown, Ford station wagon decked out with wood side-paneling (because no car is complete without wood on the exterior). My Dad made plenty of money as an executive at a Fortune 500 company, but being born at the tail end of the Great Depression in 1937, I guess he didn't feel he could justify spending money on cars.

He finally relented and bought a used school-bus orange, two-door Vega.

In fact, for a while, it was only a one-door vehicle. The driver's side door hinges didn't function fully or consistently (something you tend to expect from a hinge). They had rusted out and the door had a bad habit of falling off when opened. Instead of getting it repaired right away, my Dad tied a rope through the door and over the roof and back to secure it, rolling up the window to cinch it as tight as possible. Since he couldn't open his door, he had to climb over the stick shift, over the passenger seat, and get out of the passenger side door.

Mind you, he had a reserved parking spot with his name on the sign.

At least both of the doors in my Metro worked, and it was silver. Come to think of it, what kind of car was Matt driving that made taking mine the better choice?

Matt Dorsey and I struck up a friendship when he attended one of the Unlimited Power weekend seminars I conducted as part of the Anthony Robbins franchise I owned at the time. "Sensei" Matt owned two Karate dojos. I had trained in Tae Kwon Do for eight years and was looking for something different. Well, truth be told, the instructor at the Tae Kwon Do dojang had forbidden me from sparring. He said I was too rough, that some of the students had complained.

Having wrestled in high school and college before moving on to full contact sparring, I probably trained with a level of intensity that was more than what the typical student bargained for. Actually it was a little more than I bargained for at times too, having been on the receiving end of a broken cheekbone, a few cracked ribs, and busted up fingers and toes.

Whatever. Tape it up and walk it off.

Soon after meeting Matt at the Unlimited Power weekend, I began training with him in stick fighting and later Karate.

Sensei Matt frequently sponsored and attended training camps with instructors from many different styles. He was planning to attend the Northeastern Martial Arts Conference at Wells College and invited me along. The camp was hosted by Kevin Seaman and featured four instructors: Muay Thai boxing instructor Ajarn Surachai "Chai" Sirisute, who had a 63 – 0 professional record when he fought in Thailand; Guro Larry Hartsell, a former student of Bruce Lee who was teaching grappling; martial arts legend Guro Dan Inosanto, who was teaching the Filipino martial art of Kali/Escrima; and Sifu Francis Fong, considered by many to be one of the finest Wing Chun instructors in the U.S.A.

We reached Wells College and registered. The conference was four days, but we had signed up only for the first day due to our busy schedules and prior commitments.

The first session of the day was Muay Thai. I considered myself to be in pretty good shape and figured I'd handle it no problem.

I was wrong.

I completely soaked through two T-shirts and after the session felt like I had been in a fight and lost. Badly.

My back and hamstrings felt like rocks. Donning my last dry T-shirt, I prepared for the Wing Chun session by stretching on the hardwood gym floor. While managing a feeble imitation of a split, I looked around at the 50-or-so other participants. There were a few Karate-ka there — all in their canvas gis (which produced wonderful snapping sound effects when they kicked or punched but which were painfully hot to wear). These were cinched tightly by belts — a few black, the rest brown and purple. One of the black belts was a woman with grey hair and spectacles who looked to be in her sixties.

The rest of the group was unbelted, dressed in sweatpants (a choice they were certainly regretting) or shorts, and tank tops or T-shirts. There was an entire group all wearing black sweatpants and black T-shirts or tanks, with shaved heads, goatees, and at least one visible tattoo — a few tribal bands, a dragon, and one guy who had a snarling leopard in full color leaping off the width of his back. I wondered if having a shaved head, facial hair and ink was a prerequisite for joining their school. I guess that ruled out most women.

A few minutes later, Francis Fong entered the gym. His jet-black hair was longer than in the brochure picture, falling almost to his shoulders. He was a couple inches taller than my 5'5", and dressed all in black — wrestling shoes, sweatpants, and a tank top which revealed sinewy arms, ropey with muscle like steel cable.

He moved his compact frame from his center, easily and lightly, gliding across the floor. He was quick to smile as he shook hands with each and every person. Judging by the way he greeted others so warmly, I assumed he knew them from previous camps, but when he came to me he smiled as if we were old friends. "Francis Fong," he said, extending his hand.

I was accustomed to a military style of martial arts instruction, one mandating the student bow first from a position of strict attention. I wasn't sure quite what to do. In my confusion I half stood at attention, half bowed, and uttered something that contained the word "sir."

"Call me Sifu," he said, patting my shoulder.

I shook his hand. A feeling like a mild electrical current raced up my right arm and coursed through my body. I didn't know anything about qi at the time, but as we shook, an energy and calmness suffused me, as real as if I'd slipped into a warm bath. I felt myself leaning in slightly, being drawn in by a magnetic force at once both gentle and powerful.

Sifu Fong finished greeting each student individually then moved to the center of the gym. After a brief introduction from Kevin Seaman, Sifu Fong began. His voice was flavored with the sing-song rhythm of his native Hong Kong.

"Why bother spending years and years training in martial arts? Just get a gun. A bullet is faster than a punch any day. You don't have to work out, only your trigger finger. That's it," he said grinning, pulling the trigger on an imaginary gun. "You get a black belt right away."

Everybody laughed.

"The answer is that even though you may never get into a fight, you are always fighting yourself. That's the only real fight."

No one laughed.

"A lot of people start practicing martial arts because they want to kick someone's butt, or they don't want to get their butt kicked," he said, panning the room, his face unlined. "But, later on, it changes."

I quickly learned that Sifu Fong had a gift for integrating humor and profundity, fluidly slipping between the two, getting you to drop your guard then delivering the knockout punch. His combinations were dead-on target

"Really, what does it matter? Self-defense is good. Being healthy is good, too. But if you aren't at peace with yourself, what does it really matter?"

He paused to let the message sink in.

"Use your training to help your life."

"The goal of the martial arts is not for the destruction of an opponent but rather for self-growth and self-perfection."

Guro Dan Inosanto

LESSON 2
BE YOUR BEST

*Whenever you compare yourself to other people,
you think either you are better, or not as good.
That way is a trap.
It will never be enough to fill your emptiness.
The more you run after it, the more you will need.
It will never be enough because you will never be enough.
You will do better than others; others will do better than you.
Who cares? Just be your best. Be happy with who you are.*

"Take a look around you. Who is the best here?"

I swore I could hear the sound of chests inflating (although I couldn't be sure, as it was hard to hear over the sound of my own chest inflating).

"You are, Sifu," someone answered.

He laughed. "Don't try to be better than somebody else. Don't try to be the best. Whenever you do that, then you have to compare yourself to other people. Then, you think either you are better, or not as good."

I exhaled.

"You think you're tough? There's always someone tougher than you," he said shaking his head. "You think you're strong? Always someone stronger. You think you're crazy? Go to a mental hospital. I tell you, there are a lot of people crazier than you."

I was pretty sure he was looking at the guys with the shaved heads and goatees.

"That way is not the answer. It will never be enough to fill your emptiness. The more you run after it, the more you will need. That way is a trap. It will never be enough because you will never be enough."

He looked in my direction and my stomach knotted. Just minutes before, I was comparing myself to everyone else there, looking for weaknesses, assessing how they stood, where they held tension in their bodies, gauging their reach.

Ultimately, I was wondering how I measured up.

At that point in my life, a year shy of 30, I hadn't quite worked through all of my testosterone issues, and it showed more than I would have liked.

"That way is never enough because you are never enough," he repeated, looking around.

"Instead of trying to be *the* best, concentrate on being *your* best. Be happy for yourself. But be happy for others, too. You'll do better than somebody else. Others will do better than you. Who cares? I don't really care if you are better than someone else. I care that you keep getting better than you were before," he said.

Sifu paused, and nodded slightly as if to underscore the point. "Just be your best. Be happy with who you are."

"There is nothing noble about feeling superior to others.
True nobility comes from being better than your former self.

Hindu Proverb

Sifu Fong, Ajarn Chai Sirisute, Simo Tracey Fong, Guro Dan Inosanto

LESSON 3
NO ONE CAN GIVE YOU WHAT YOU DON'T HAVE

If you aren't happy with yourself,
you'll never make anyone else happy either.
No one can give you what you don't have for yourself.
You'll always be looking to get something from other people
to make you feel a certain way.

"Some teachers talk about their students — my student is this champion, my other student is that champion. If you feel good about yourself, then you won't go around bragging how much better you are than someone else.

"That's why I don't even like the word 'master'. *Sifu* is better. Sifu means both father and teacher. You have to take responsibility for your student like you would a son or daughter. You have to love your student like you would your own son or daughter."

Sifu Fong continued talking for a number of minutes before he began any physical training. One guy over in the corner was circling his hips and shaking out his legs. He was either tight from the previous training or anxious to "get to it." If so, he was unaware that the most valuable lessons Sifu would teach were not embedded in technique.

When Sifu Fong did progress to the physical training, his hands were a blur. Lightning fast, much faster than anything I had ever seen by orders of magnitude.

As impressive as that was though, the speed of his movements and the mastery of his technique weren't what remained after the session was over; it was the sense of inner peace and energy that radiated from him, and the truth in his words.

"Every one of you has a gift. Your job is to bring that gift forward.

Maybe that gift will be in martial arts. People think they can master a lot of different things. Honestly, that's impossible. I don't think it can be done. Maybe one art can be mastered, if you are persistent, but not multiple arts.

"If you want to be a master of anything, a martial art, playing an instrument, business, singing, or painting, it takes a long time and a lot of practice. Years. Years," he repeated. "There are no shortcuts. Believe me," he said with a quick shake of his head and a shrug.

"Anyway, what difference does it make how many people you can knock out if you're not happy? Nobody cares. If you aren't happy with yourself, you'll never make anyone else happy either."

I felt numb. At that point in my life, I was confusing achievement with happiness. I had the mistaken notion that achieving more would make me happy.

And it did, for a fleeting moment — wrestling championships, black belts, full contact fight wins, an Ivy League degree, business success. But for some reason, I could never seem to stay in the present and enjoy what I had worked so hard to achieve. Those feelings evaporated like morning mist as I sought happiness in yet something else, somewhere down the road. I was caught in the *when / then* web. *When* I get — (whatever, it was always shifting) — *then* I'll be happy, always thinking that the next goal would be *it*.

What I didn't realize was that whatever I achieved in life would never make me happy, no matter what it was. And nothing or no one, as Sifu said, could give me that sense of inner peace and fulfillment if I didn't find it myself.

"You'll always be looking to get something from other people to make you feel a certain way. Really," he went on to say, "no one can give you what you don't have for yourself."

It would take me a long time to learn that lesson.

*"What you get won't make you happy.
Who you become will make you happy."*

Anthony Robbins

22

LESSON 4
MASTER YOURSELF

*Mastering an art is really about mastering yourself.
If you haven't mastered yourself,
it doesn't matter if you master something else.*

"It's funny," Sifu said. "People get so caught up in things that don't matter. People ask me, *'Is Wing Chun a hard or soft style?'* I say it's soft, until you get hit, then it's hard!

"People argue over which martial art is the best. The truth is that no one martial art is better than another. Different styles are good for different things. It depends on the situation.

"An art is different than a physical workout," Sifu continued. "Art is never done. When will you be done? When you are in your coffin, then you'll be done. That's why not many people really want to learn the art. Mastering an art is really about mastering yourself — about putting yourself into it, discovering your own way, your own style. Ultimately, your art should help you become aware of yourself, to gain insight into yourself."

For him, it seemed, art and life were intertwined, each representing and flowing into the other. Art wasn't something you did. Rather, it was the full expression of who you were, a canvas upon which to exhibit your essence.

His comments made me think deeply about what I really wanted. *What was I seeking through my training? What did mastering an art mean? What did mastering myself mean?* There was certainly a physical aspect in terms of mastering technique and timing — but it went far beyond that. I'd met many people who were physically and technically gifted who didn't, in my mind, exemplify mastery. To me mastery incorporated a flowing, relaxed way of moving, of being fully present and totally absorbed in the moment, all while being keenly aware of one's surroundings. Mastery contained stillness, centeredness, and sinking — it embodied a sense of inner peace and a clarity of thinking, a blend of humility and confidence, and an acceptance of the way things are, while simultaneously striving to grow and improve. Mastery was an amalgamation of proficiency in the realms of physical, emotional, mental, and spiritual awareness.

"It's more important to master yourself, and definitely much harder. If you haven't mastered yourself, it doesn't matter if you master something else."

I regretted not signing up for all four days.

> *"Knowing others is intelligence;*
> *knowing yourself is true wisdom,*
> *Mastering others is strength;*
> *mastering yourself is true power."*
>
> Lao-tzu, Tao te Ching

24

LESSON 5
RELAX, BE LIKE A KID

You have to relax.
Otherwise, you'll never learn.
That's why I'm always telling stories and jokes.
I want you to relax and enjoy yourself and breathe.
When you breathe fully and take your time, you relax.
By relaxing, you can learn better.

At the camp I had taken notes on a number of exercises, complete with quickly-sketched pictures of hand and body positions. Every day in the months that followed I took out my leather bound journal and studied and drilled those exercises over and over. I didn't know if I was doing the movements correctly or not since it was so different than the martial arts I had studied until then. But whatever I lacked for in technique I made up for in enthusiasm.

It reminded me of when I was 12 years old and took a self-defense book out of the library. My brothers and I poured over the pictures of various stances, kicks and hand attacks. We practiced the movements with the zeal of young boys, inspired by a poster of Bruce Lee taped to our bedroom wall, convinced we would soon be like the *Little Dragon*. At some point, we wanted to hit something besides the air, so we made a heavy bag by filling an old canvas Army duffel with dirt. It took all three of us to hang it on our chin up bar — two of us to lift it up and one to attach it. The thing must have weighed 200 pounds.

I was the first to try it out. I got into my horse stance and chambered my right fist, palm up. My left arm was extended, palm down, into a tight fist. Per the book I yelled "Ki-yah!" and punched with everything I had.

I tore the skin off two of my knuckles and nearly broke my wrist.

My brothers both doubled over with laughter.

I rubbed my wrist and regrouped. In lieu of bag gloves, which we didn't own, I stuck my hands into two pairs of white athletic tube socks. They looked silly and didn't offer much in the way of padding, but they did soak up the blood. My mother was no doubt confused when she found them in the laundry.

I was hoping my Wing Chun efforts would turn out a little better.

Towards the middle of the fall, I received a flyer in the mail for a seminar with Francis Fong. Kevin Seaman was bringing him to Cortland for a two day event dedicated solely to Wing Chun. I filled out the registration and sent in my fee the same day I received it.

On the first day of the seminar, I awoke at 6:00 a.m. to make the two-hour drive from Rochester to Cortland, New York. I mentally rehearsed the movements as I drove and arrived at Sifu Kevin's East/West Martial Arts Academy with an hour to spare.

Kevin's school was a stand-alone building off a main thorough-fare, his logo displayed prominently on the outside signage as well as the glass window front. There was only one other car there when I arrived and I parked next to it. I grabbed my bag and entered through the glass double-doors into a large linoleum tiled space. There was a registration table set up at the front, next to the Pro Shop, which was fully stocked with Kali sticks, focus mitts, Thai pads, shin guards, shirts, and other martial arts equipment. One of his students was there taking registrations.

After signing the required forms, I ventured into the main training area in the back. It was 50 by 150 feet, converted from a four-bay quick oil change franchise. Fluorescent lights perched high above on steel I-beams illuminated the gray cinderblock walls.

An elevated boxing ring took up most of the far right corner. Two regular-sized heavy bags and a full-length Thai heavy bag, six feet long and just inches off the floor, hung to the left of the entrance. Containers full of Kali sticks stood nearby and an oak Wing Chun wooden dummy was mounted against the far wall. The remainder of the space was open, covered with maroon wrestling mats.

The overall feel was of an old school boxing gym — gritty and raw. All it needed was a guy chomping on a cigar in the corner reading the paper with a towel slung over his shoulder. The kind of guy who wouldn't look up when you said "hi" and who definitely would not return the greeting.

After a while other martial artists started showing up. I introduced myself and chatted with a few of them while continuing to warm up.

Kevin Seaman and Sifu Fong arrived a few minutes before 10:00 a.m. Sifu bowed at the entrance of the gym and stowed his bag off to the side. He looked even more relaxed and vibrant than I remembered. As before, he made the rounds to greet everyone, shaking each hand and hugging a few people. "Good to see you again," he said to me, shaking hands. I felt the same surge of energy as before — that calming, magnetic force. I didn't know what to call it, but I knew it was something I wanted.

"Good to see you, Sifu," I said sans half-bow.

Sensei Matt couldn't make the seminar so I partnered with someone I met there. We started with a movement Sifu had demonstrated back in the summer—one I had practiced religiously since, a bong sao lop sao drill. I smoothly intercepted my partner's fist and quickly pulled his wrist, followed in succession by a knife hand and punch.

Then Sifu came by. Because, for some reason, I felt like I had to perform, my shoulders and upper back turned into blocks of wood. My movements were tense and rushed. He observed and gently corrected. A few minutes later he called for everyone's attention.

"Listen up. One thing so important is to relax. Wing Chun was created by a woman, so you need to take your time, relax, and take it easy. But, like a woman, if she gets mad, watch out!" he chuckled.

"As you gain experience, you relax more, just like driving a car. In the beginning, when you first are learning, you are tense. You know how it is. You adjust the mirrors. You make sure nobody is talking. You want everything to be quiet so that you concentrate," he said, miming the antics of an inexperienced driver.

"But after a while, you get used to driving and you relax. You start to do all these other things at the same time—eating, listening to music, putting on make-up."

We all laughed when he pretended to apply mascara.

"But if you get in a new car, it takes a little while to get used to it, so the tension can creep back up a little bit. Most of you have a lot of experience in your own style, like driving your own car. But this is like a new car to you, so it will take a while. Always try to relax."

We resumed our practice and again I executed well. So well, that Sifu asked me to demonstrate in front of the class.

Then, in front of everyone, not so well.

Crap.

I didn't grasp how important it was to approach Wing Chun with a sense of relaxation, without tension, without thinking.

He stopped and explained the movement to us once more.

"He was doing it before," my partner explained.

Sifu nodded knowingly. "It's different when everyone is watching, right? It's like kissing your girlfriend. At first you are nervous. Now, you aren't nervous, unless your wife is watching," he said grinning.

"Listen up," Sifu said to the group. "Be like a kid. Kids don't care. They make a mistake and have fun, but they learn so much. We think we have to be perfect and if we aren't, we get all tense."

Ah, perfection. My nemesis.

"Don't worry so much and you'll learn it. Focus on one thing at a time. Learn little by little and relax. Have fun. If you have fun while you practice, then you are more likely to keep up and continue. You'll be willing to devote the time that it takes to get good. It takes a lot of time and a lot of hits. If each time you get hit you think, *"Oh no. I'm no good. I'll never amount to anything,"* you won't want to continue. You'll get down on yourself and feel lousy. Then you won't feel good about practicing, then you will dread it, then you will quit.

"Go lighter. Take it easy. Have fun," he concluded.

During the entire weekend, Sifu never told anyone to go faster or speed up. Even though he possessed, arguably, some of the fastest hands in the world, he kept telling us to "take our time," and to "get used to it." Sifu stressed the importance of relaxing the mind first, then the body. From there, one could move freely, unencumbered by a judgmental mind and tense body. He knew that we would speed up when we were ready.

"Go slow, be smooth. Then you can be fast. Don't think about being fast at the beginning. Go slow, take your time, and get the movement down. Make sure you are smooth and can flow. If you can do it slowly and smoothly, you will get fast. Don't worry about it."

Later that day he came over to me and my partner. "Good. You are doing good," he said, patting me on the shoulder. "You have to relax. Otherwise, you'll never learn. That's why I'm always telling stories and jokes. I want you to relax and enjoy yourselves and breathe. If you are tense, you hold your breath. If you don't breathe, I don't think you will relax," he kidded.

"When you breathe fully and take your time, you relax. By relaxing, you can learn better. Just like a kid."

He told the group that Wing Chun is different than a lot of other martial arts. Back in Hong Kong, classes were held in the Sifu's apartment. People would come and go. No set class times. During practice, people would stop and take a break to have some water or tea. The Sifus would sometimes drink wine before they did a sticking hands exercise called chi-sao to help them relax so that they could develop their sensitivity.

"You can't develop sensitivity if you are tense," he told us.

"Wing Chun is different. It's not this," he said, dropping down in a deep front stance and executing a low block and straight punch, his fists clenched and muscles straining. He stood back up. "I'm not saying Wing Chun is better," he said, pausing for a moment before adding, "I'm just saying this is Wing Chun.

"Don't worry about hitting. Take your time. Learn to relax. Like T'ai Chi. If you get that, then the rest will come. If you don't, don't worry about hitting. Someone will knock you out first."

"There are 5 aspects of practicing T'ai Chi.
First, you calm down.
Second, you eliminate any exertion.
Third, you try to be consistent, neither fast nor slow,
no intervals in between.
The fourth ... is to truly and precisely practice,
[and] to study the proper movements of the body.
The fifth is perseverance."

T'ai Chi Ch'uan Sifu Ma Yeuh Liang

LESSON 6
SINK

You want to be strong?
Be like water — relaxed.
When you relax, you sink down into the ground.
No one is smarter than heaven,
no one is stronger than the earth.
We are in between.
Relax into the earth.
Let him fight himself.
Don't fight against him.

We switched partners to practice entry to takedown to ground sub-mission. I partnered with Eric Winfree, a long time martial artist and instructor out of Syracuse NY, by way of Texas.

"This is amazing," he said, in a voice much softer than I expected for his size.

I did the entry — a slapping hand (pak sao) to a neck chop (sut sao) — followed by a low cutting punch to a neck lock and foot sweep. I was having trouble reaching around Eric's neck because he didn't really have one. It was merged with trapezius muscles which would have looked entirely appropriate on one of those bulls from his home state. His step-brother and two cousins played in the NFL. Put a uniform on him and Eric would have fit right in.

I managed to take him down by sweeping out his tree trunk of a leg. He landed in a way that made an arm bar the best follow up. I put my left leg over his throat, cinched my right foot against his ribs to keep him from moving, pinched my knees together, and pulled his wrist towards me. His arm was about the same size as my leg, but I had his elbow positioned just right for an arm bar so when I arched my hips he tapped out.

"Really nice," he said, again in the soft voice.

He went next. He moved quickly, again more so than I had expected for his size, and took me down with the same movement I used, though with less trouble finding my neck since I actually have one. Unfortunately for me, the way I landed meant that his best follow up was a side neck crank / choke. Eric clasped his hands together and squeezed. At the same time he got up on his toes and shifted his weight over my chest.

All the air whooshed out of my lungs. I heard a couple crunches and hoped that my ribs were still more or less where they should be. My hands were otherwise occupied, so I tapped my foot on the mat.

He released his grip and got up.

"Nice," I said, also in a soft voice, but not because that was my normal one. "What do you weigh?"

"285."

I nodded, partly in recognition of his statement and partly to make sure my neck still worked.

That explained a few things. He only had 135 pounds on me.

After ten minutes of drilling that exercise, Sifu Fong called for everyone to stop and focus on the center of the room. He looked over to Eric and put his hands together in front of his forehead as a sign of respect. It was the salutation used in Muay Thai. Sifu Fong was an Instructor in Muay Thai and was recognized as the Director of the Southeastern Region for the Thai Boxing Association of the U.S.A., under the direction of Ajarn Chai Sirisute. He used that salutation as often as the Gin Lai Wing Chun salutation, the palm and fist from a cat stance.

"Sir, can I use you?" Sifu asked Eric.

Eric returned the gesture of respect and trotted to the center of the room where Sifu was standing.

"No matter how strong somebody is, I don't think anyone can lift a waterbed," Sifu Fong began. "Do you? Have you seen these strong man competitions? They lift refrigerators, logs, big chains, but I've never seen anyone lift a waterbed."

His stance was casual, as if having a friendly conversation. He nonchalantly extended his hand towards Eric and asked him to push on him as hard as he could.

This will be interesting, I thought.

Eric got down low, dug his feet into the mat, and pushed for all he was worth.

Sifu sank his 150-pound frame down a couple of inches, and raised one knee to waist height. Eric kept pushing, the beads of perspiration breaking on his head, but Sifu just laughed as he calmly balanced on one leg. "You want to be strong? Be like water — relaxed."

What the ....? I could have used this information about 10 minutes ago. Actually, I could have used this information years ago. My high school wrestling coach used to say, "Anything works if you do it hard enough." In the same vein, my college wrestling coach told us, "You can never be too strong." I disagreed and said I had wrestled guys who were too strong.

"If you are tense, you are like ice." He tensed his body and Eric pushed him over easily.

Ice, ice baby.

Sifu resumed his casual stance and called two other students to join Eric. They weren't quite as big as Eric, but they were still a lot bigger than Sifu. And they were both from Eric's school in Syracuse which, of course, meant they had shaved heads and goatees.

Sifu extended his hand and all three dug in and pushed. Though they strained mightily, they couldn't budge him even an inch.

No way.

He remained entrenched in his one-legged position, rooted to the ground, as solid as a giant oak. The more they strained, the harder he laughed.

After a minute or so of all-out effort, the three were exhausted and dripping with sweat. He excused them, much to their relief.

"When you relax, you sink down into the ground. Then, what are they pushing?"

"The ground," a few people answered.

"No one is smarter than heaven, no one is stronger than the earth. We are in between. Relax into the earth. Let him fight himself. Don't fight against him. Don't use your muscles. I don't have much muscle, so I just use my bones. Let your partner push against the ground. If he can push the ground you better run away."

"The cyclone derives its powers from a calm center. So does a person."

Norman Vincent Peale

LESSON 7
DON'T RESIST, REDIRECT

Where does water go, above or below?
Below, to the lowest level.
To redirect their energy, you have to go lower.
You have to put yourself below others.
When it comes to you, don't try to go over it.
Go below it, accept what he gives you, and redirect it back.

How could he do that? I wondered. How could Sifu resist what must have been hundreds, if not thousands of pounds of force coming from three different directions?

I asked him.

"I didn't resist it," he said. "If you resist it, you can't do it."

Uh-hmmm. I nodded and looked down, as if the answer were somewhere on the floor. It certainly wasn't in my head or my body.

He knew I didn't quite grasp it. "First, you have to sink your energy down. Think of a little kid that doesn't want to be picked up. You ever try that? This little kid might weigh thirty pounds, but he sinks down and you can't lift him. He feels like a hundred pounds and you think, 'What the hell is this kid eating? How did he get so heavy?'"

I exhaled forcefully in an attempt to empty my upper body of its perennial tension and allowed myself to sink into the ground.

He asked me to put out my hand just like he did in the demonstration. "Now, when I push, try to stop me."

I tried to stop him, and got pushed back instantly.

Hadn't I sunk down?

He asked me to try again, but this time he used only his pinkie to push.

Still, I was sent flying backwards.

This isn't too humiliating. I got pushed back by one finger. A pinkie no less! Arrgggghhhh!! Oh wait. I'm supposed to be like a kid and have fun. Ha ha! Yay! Fake smile.

"Don't try to stop me. Let my energy flow through you," he said.

I pursed my lips, not quite sure how to do that.

"Take my force and then cycle it back to me," he explained.

I extended my arm and grasped his hand in mine. With his free hand he traced a path over our clasped hands, back underneath mine, and up and over his in a path similar to a bicycle chain coming towards me, then going down and back. He continued drawing the chain as he increased his pressure so that I understood how to redirect his force.

Once I got it, he pushed with both hands, digging his feet into the ground. To my surprise, I remained rooted.

He asked me to try again, but this time he drew the chain flowing the other direction. He started from the bottom and come over the top, like a bike chain in reverse.

He was only pushing with one hand, but I couldn't hold him, and was once again thrust back.

That was my introduction to qigong. Qi is the Chinese concept for life force or vital energy (and also a great Scrabble word). Qigong has a number of translations, mainly referring to cultivation of life energy. There are various methods of manipulating your own or another's energy or qi. In this case, qigong referred to my ability to control the direction of the combined energy of myself and my partner. "But I was letting your force come," I said, confused. "I didn't resist it."

He smiled knowingly and asked me what the difference was.

I wasn't sure.

"Where does water go, above or below?" he asked.

"Below, to the lowest level."

"To redirect, you have to go lower. You have to put yourself below others."

He took my hand and placed my arm into the outstretched position. "When it comes to you, don't try to go over it," he said, tracing the flow of the circle so that my force was on top of his — the reverse bicycle chain.

Don't try to beat him, in other words.

"Go below it, accept what he gives you, and redirect it back," tracing the flow the other way.

Accept.

It was working, so he asked two other students to push on my hand as he drew the bicycle chain flow around them and me, bigger and bigger. He got another person to push, all the while making the flow of the chain larger and larger until it encompassed the space behind the three of them and behind me. They dug their feet into the mat and grunted, their faces turning red as they strained forward. To me, it didn't feel like they were pushing at all.

The rest of the class watched, and ended up applauding.

I broke into a confused smile.

"If I can do it, you can do it, too. Don't just believe me, try it for yourself."

"You have to put yourself below others."

Sifu Francis Fong

LESSON 8

THE HARDER YOU TRY, THE WORSE YOU DO

*In martial arts, if you try to kill your partner on every shot,
you won't understand the basics.
It will be very difficult for you to acquire the sensitivity and
timing you need to get really good.
When you train, go easy at first.
Later, when you have the technique,
you can speed up and the power will be there.
In a lot of things, the harder you try, the better you do.
But in Wing Chun, this is not really true.
The harder you try, the worse you do.*

It still didn't make sense to my analytical mind. Later, during a break,
I asked Sifu for more clarification. "What do you think about when
they're pushing on you?"

He shook his head quickly. "You can't think. If you think, then you
are stopping. It won't come natural."

For him it was probably like trying to describe what a food tasted
like to someone who had never tried it.

"You have to stay in the moment and let things happen. Like
watching water flow in a river, you go along with it. You don't really
think about it, right?"

"No, sir."

"Don't concentrate on yourself. Pay attention to them, where they
are coming from, and what they are doing."

He made it sound so easy. But his ability was the result of decades
of study and practice in not just technique, but in relaxing, sinking,
letting go, and not resisting. By placing himself below others and seeking to accept and understand, rather than control, he cultivated a level
of sensitivity that was mind boggling.

I had read stories of ancient martial arts masters who were so sensitive that a fly couldn't land on them. Up until that point I had considered those as merely fables.

Come to think of it, I'd never seen a fly land on Sifu. Maybe those stories were true.

Okay, then, the lessons were to relax, sink down, empty myself of my own desires and reactions, not think, and focus on others.

Just those five things.

Simultaneously.

While cultivating a reservoir of intensity and explosive power that could take someone out in a blink of an eye.

Wasn't there another way? I wondered.

There was, actually. I had tried that for quite some time, but it hadn't yielded the results I wanted.

My ego was really unhappy.

The group resumed training. A few of the participants were going full bore, both tense and intense. After a while Sifu called everyone back to the center of the training floor.

"In martial arts, if you try to kill your partner on every shot, you won't understand the basics. It will be very difficult for you to acquire the sensitivity and timing you need to get really good. Not to mention, no one will want to work out with you."

I noticed a few sheepish grins. But not nearly enough.

"When you train, go easy at first. Later, when you have the technique, you can speed up and the power will be there. But don't be tense. Don't rush or you will lose your technique and your power, and all of your friends."

For some reason I thought back to two things Tony Robbins once told me. The first was that our stress ultimately points out our deepest fear, and that a common deep fear is that we aren't good enough.

Was I afraid that I wasn't good enough? Was the reason I rushed or tensed up because I wanted to feel strong?

Maybe I didn't believe that just relaxing and using position was enough. But hadn't I just seen Sifu prove that it had? Hadn't I just proven that?

The other thing Tony said to me was, "Your vulnerability is your power."

Could being open and relaxed — some would say vulnerable — really be my power? Could it be everyone's power? The Tao te Ching, Lao-Tzu's well-known book of ancient wisdom said:

The soft overcomes the hard, and the weak the strong.
Everyone knows this is true, but few can put it into practice.

By relaxing, sinking and grounding, by letting energy flow through him, Sifu epitomized these sage words.

"In a lot of things, the harder you try, the better you do. But in Wing Chun, this is not really true," Sifu said.

Virtually all of my successes up until that point — in wrestling, martial arts, school and professional life — had been due to working hard — harder than anyone else, or so I thought.

These concepts threw me for a loop.

Everyone knows this is true.

"The harder you try, the worse you do." He paused to let that sink in.

But few can put it into practice.

A mistake I was making... ONE of the mistakes I was making, was trying to achieve relaxation through effort, as if relaxation was something to be acquired, rather than something to be uncovered by letting go.

"Some people call Wing Chun combat T'ai Chi. Practice like T'ai Chi," Sifu said. "What you need is consistency, persistence and no resistance."

"Tension is who you think you should be.
Relaxation is who you are."

Chinese proverb

Eric Winfree and Sifu Fong – Martial Arts America, Rochester NY

LESSON 9
LET YOURSELF MAKE MISTAKES

Let yourself make mistakes.
We learn more from our mistakes.
But you can't learn from a mistake until you make a mistake.
When you train, don't worry about winning.
In training make sure you learn as you go along, little by little.
1,000 out of 1,000 times you lose.
Then you lose 999 times out of 1,000, then 998.
Slowly, consistently, you learn.

After four hours of training at a seminar in Cortland, New York one Saturday afternoon a few years later, roughly 30 fellow students and I joined Sifu for dinner at a Chinese restaurant. Nestled in a row of stores in a nearby shopping mall, we pushed together a few small tables to form one long row, taking up the entire place. Even though everyone ordered separately, we ended up sharing dishes family style.

"How long have you been studying martial arts, Sifu?" Bryan from St. Catherine's, Ontario Canada asked while we waited for our food.

"I started training when I was a baby, in diapers," he said, grinning. "I started when I was twelve. I first trained in Judo, then Tae Kwon Do for a little while. I liked Judo. I threw people around. Then they put me with guys much heavier than me. Oh, I tell you," he said laughing, "I hurt my shoulder, my legs, then I didn't like Judo no more.

"Every day in school there was a fight. If there was no fight, it was like no day. Every day we would know when and where the fight was. I got into a fight and went to pull the guy's shirt like a gi. I went to a Catholic school so we all wore dress shirts and ties. I grabbed the guy's shirt to throw him and it ripped right off. I thought, *Oh no, my judo's not working*," he said, again laughing.

41

"One day at school I see a guy finish a fight in three seconds. 'What's that?' I asked. I found out it was Wing Chin. I wanted that.

"In 1965 I began training in Wing Chun under Sifu Jiu Wan." Francis Fong was accepted into a closed-door school led by Sifu Jiu Wan, a well-known instructor who had immigrated to Hong Kong from Southern China. Jiu Wan and Yip Man, considered by many to be the father of Modern Wing Chun as well as Bruce Lee's Wing Chun instructor, studied martial arts together at the Jing Mo Guen in Foshan.

Jing Mo Guen was considered one of the most elite institutions in southern China, dedicated solely to the highest levels of martial arts training. Yip Man left early, completing the Wing Chun system elsewhere, and was the first to teach Wing Chun in Hong Kong. Sifu Jiu Wan went on to become a teacher at the Jing Mo Guen. When the communists came to China, Sifu Jiu Wan went to Hong Kong and joined Yip Man's organization.

Sifu Fong described his early training under Sifu Jiu Wan as very traditional and old-fashioned, with a lot of chi sao, or sticky hands training.

"In Hong Kong, training is not like here, believe me. Six months, only do Siu Nim Tao. Sifus don't teach too much. They sit down, drink, smoke, maybe yell something," he said, laughing, "Senior students teaching. My friend here asked me, 'Francis, why you work so hard? Just sit back. Relax.' I tell you, in U.S. I have to work much harder," he said.

"You don't ask any questions. Everything is 'Yes, sir!' If you say, 'No sir, I don't really understand,' you get smacked," he said, hitting the air. "'Oh,' he joked, 'Yes, Sifu. Now I got it.'"

In China, it was viewed as disrespectful to ask questions. Instructors would tell you what you needed to know when you were ready. If you asked a question, an instructor would take it to mean that you were challenging their teaching ability.

Many years later, I was in China on business speaking with an employee who was three levels down from me organizationally. She was a bright woman — she had an M.B.A. — yet appeared nervous upon entering the room, even though we had met a couple times before. I asked her why. She said that I ask a lot of questions about what she and her colleagues think, and in school they were never asked for their opinion and were taught to never question. They were taught to listen and do. "If you asked a question you were viewed as a trouble boy or trouble girl," she told me.

I was glad Sifu didn't see us as trouble.

"Sifu, what is the biggest thing that prevents people from learning Wing Chun?" I asked.

He paused so long before responding that I thought he hadn't heard me. I was about to repeat the question when he answered.

"Two things," he said. "First, not letting yourself make mistakes, and second, trying too hard."

That certainly wasn't the answer I expected. He must have sensed my surprise because he elaborated.

"We want to do something perfectly right away, right?"

I agreed.

"But do you learn more from your mistakes or your successes?"

"Mistakes," I answered.

He nodded. "Exactly. We learn more from our mistakes. But you can't learn from a mistake until you make a mistake."

That meant not just listening or thinking about it. It meant going out and trying new things with new people. Invariably you would make a mistake, meaning you get hit, but it was then that you learned — as long as your ego could deal with it.

"Nobody likes to get hit. Everyone bleeds. Only in the movies people don't get hit. But if you never get hit, you'll never learn. The trick is to keep going and try new things."

The other trick, I thought, is to associate getting hit as learning and progressing instead of as failure. In other words, getting hit is not failure; not learning from getting hit is.

"When you train, don't worry about winning. In training make sure you learn. Sometimes you win, sometimes you lose. Some days are good, some days are bad. It doesn't matter as long as you learn as you go along, little by little. 1,000 times out of 1,000 times you lose. Then you lose 999 times out of 1,000, then 998. Slowly, consistently, you learn."

"Experience is the name everyone gives to their mistakes."

Oscar Wilde

Sifu Francis Fong as a young man

LESSON 10
LEARN FROM ANYONE

Train with different people in different situations.
It doesn't matter what skill level they are.
You can learn from anyone.
You will see your own mistakes in somebody else;
the ones you point out are really your own.
The more things you try with different people,
the more you will understand and be able to apply.

He continued talking about the importance of learning and taking your time. Someone at the table said that we all knew we should go slowly, but few did. I was as guilty as the next guy.

Sifu said in nature, growth is gradual. It takes time. It can't be forced.

"What are you in such a hurry for anyway?" he asked, rhetorically. "Don't worry if it takes a long time to learn. The longer it takes to learn, the longer it will stay with you.

Then Wing Chun is going to stay with me for a lifetime, I thought, *since learning this is taking forever.*

"It is not just something for your mind to grasp. You have to understand it with your entire body. There's an old saying: 'Hear, and I forget. See, and I remember. Do, and I understand. You have to be able to do. You need to learn what to do and what not to do.'"

Someone asked Sifu what year he left Hong Kong to come to the United States. He told us that he first came to attend college in Canada in 1971 and later moved to New York. "Everyone told me that I could get a part time job to pay for college, but it wasn't really true. I ran out of money for tuition," he said laughing. "I couldn't pay my bill. The college kept asking me when I was going to pay and I kept saying, 'Soon!'"

He moved to Connecticut then New York and worked in restaurants for next to nothing — a dollar or two an hour. The restaurant owners knew he was there on a student visa so he couldn't really do much about it.

"I also moved furniture in Chinatown. Just me to bring things up three flights of stairs. One time I had to bring a mattress up three flights by myself. People think I got all my body mechanics from Wing Chun. It's from moving!" he joked.

While in New York he trained with his Wing Chun brother Jason Lau who had also emigrated from Hong Kong. In 1976, Sifu moved to Atlanta where he opened the Francis Fong Martial Arts Academy.

"So when you came to Atlanta, Sifu, who did you train with?" I asked.

"A little with Jason, but not too much. We would kill each other," he laughed. "We are like brothers. Mostly I trained with my students."

"You must have been a lot better than them, though. How did you learn?"

He shrugged. "You can learn from anyone, and you will see your mistakes in somebody else. You can only see your own mistakes. The ones you point out are really your own. Anyone can be your teacher. If you only see what you want to see, and hear what you want to hear, you will miss so much.

"When you work with others, you learn a lot from them. It doesn't matter what skill level they are. That's why you should always work together with other people. It's hard to get better by yourself. You can't tell by yourself if you are getting better. You need someone else. Just like how you look. If you look in the mirror and say, *'Oh, I'm handsome. Oh, I'm really strong.'* How do you know? You need someone else to tell you, 'I'm sorry to tell you this, but you are not that good-looking!'"

One of the Canadians joked to one of his friends, no doubt something about his looks, which earned him a punch in the arm.

"I know some instructors never train with their students. I don't know how they do that. The best thing is to train with anybody. It's so important to have experiences. Try things with different people, different times and different situations. Then you will understand more things and apply more things."

"If I am through learning, I am through."

John Wooden
Coach of UCLA Basketball and 10 NCAA Championships

LESSON II
CONSTANTLY EVOLVE

You have to evolve.
Even though you are a teacher, you have to be a student.
People don't realize how much you have to keep learning.
I learn every day, try to get better every day.

Sifu took a sip of tea and set his cup down gently, his hand still cupping it as he spoke.

"You constantly have to be evolving. Some people say I am not traditional. I say, 'What means traditional? I am Chinese. I born Hong Kong. I speak Chinese. I eat more Chinese food than you. You telling me you are more traditional than me?" he asked, grimacing. "Come on."

He took another sip of tea then shook his head.

"I see people wearing old man clothes like my grandfather. Chinese people don't even wear those clothes. Like the Kung Fu slippers. We call them lazy slippers because you can just slip them on. Bruce Lee wore them and now they are Kung Fu slippers. They are no good for Kung Fu. You kick and they fall off," he said, laughing. "Maybe hit someone in the eye.

"Some aspects of traditional are good. Like wooden dummy. The design has been around for hundreds of years. Now you see different dummies — plastic, with springs," he shook his head. "I know they are expensive. Used to be three or four hundred dollars. Now what?" he asked.

He got various responses, ranging from $750 to $3,000.

"But they are an investment. They stay with you. I get divorced but my dummy never leave," he said chuckling.

"Some people say their wives don't want the dummy in the house. Makes too much noise. That's okay — you can donate to the school," he offered. "Some of my students donated their dummies to my school. Then I get them calling, 'Uh, Sifu. I've got to talk to you. Can I have my dummy back?' I say, 'You got divorced!' They say, 'How do you know?'

"Stick with traditional because it works. Some techniques have been around for thousands of years. Why? Because they work. At the same time, you have to evolve. That's why students have to cross train. You have to know how to fight against other styles."

For his Wing Chun belt tests, students perform empty hand and weapons forms, various drills and a number of strength and balance exercises, such as two knuckle push-ups and battle punches on one leg. In addition, following that, students testing for green belt and above have to go three rounds.

The first round is the Wing Chun round where the instructor will feed the student with focus mitts. Depending on the belt level, the student needs to get between 150 and 250 hits in three minutes, also demonstrating simultaneous low, middle and high parrying and striking.

The second three minute round is Muay Thai, where the student is required to get in a minimum 60 kicks and 40 knees. For the higher level testing, the feeders get to kick the student too, so the students have to shield and move in and out of range very quickly. And keep their hands up.

The third round is grappling. The student has to reverse or get free in one minute or less from their partner's top, side and rear mount positions.

Besides having to know Muay Thai and Jiu Jitsu in addition to Wing Chun, the student needs to be in good enough shape to go three rounds after what was already a rigorous test.

"Some people criticize this approach because they say it isn't traditional. They think they will never get taken to the ground. Or they can defeat a Muay Thai fighter," he shrugged.

"If you think you will never get taken down, you will get taken down," he said, nodding. "If you think you will never get choked out, someone gonna choke you out. You afraid of getting punched, you will get punched," he said with a smirk.

"Same time, if you never train Muay Thai, how do you know how they will come at you? If you never train on the ground, how do you know what to do?" Sifu asked. "Plus, it makes you humble. You get kicked in the thigh with a Muay Thai kick, you walk around limping for a week. Every step, Muay Thai, Muay Thai, Muay Thai. You get choked out, every time you breathe, BJJ, BJJ, BJJ. You get bil jee in the eye, every time you blink, Wing Chun, Wing Chun, Wing Chun.

"Even though you are a teacher, you have to be a student. People don't realize how much you have to keep learning. I learn every day, try to get better every day. Even if I'm flying, I am training in my mind. Visualizing," he said, leaning back in his chair.

"Look at Guro Dan," he said as he sat forward again, referring to Dan Inosanto. "He is incredible. Every day he is learning. He is so excited, like a kid. I did something and he says to me, 'Sifu that is incredible.' I say, 'Guro, you showed that to me!'"

Someone asked Sifu how he met Guro Dan. In 1981 Sifu Fong was asked by film coordinator Bobby Bass to help choreograph the fight scenes for the movie Sharkey's Machine starring Burt Reynolds. It was during this filming that he met up with Guro Dan, which led to a lifelong friendship and a sharing of their mutual respect and interest in the martial arts.

Guro Dan was in Atlanta for two months. "It's not like today where they fly you in for a couple days, do your thing, and then fly back out. Back then we were there for two months. Most days nothing to do but wait, so that's where I learned Kali and got exposed to Ajarn Chai.

"One day Guro Dan was hurt, so Burt Reynolds asked me if I could step in on a scene where I'd play the bad guy and attack him. Burt was a big star," he said laughing. "'What specifically do you mean?' I asked.

"Burt says, 'Jump me!' He wanted me to jump him from up on a ledge. Burt was a tough guy and I think he thought he would catch me. I ask, 'Are you sure?' Burt says, 'Give me everything you got!' So I jump down with all my weight. Wham! Burt goes down right on the concrete floor, blood pouring from his nose. The set goes completely quiet, people rush up to him with a towel. I'm so scared, I thought I hurt the big star," he said laughing.

"Burt gets up, he's pretty tough. They ask if he wants to take a break. He wipes his nose and throws the towel away. 'Again!' he yells. This time I think I better go easy. So I jump again, a little more gently, and he catches me and throws me down on the concrete. No padding, no nothing. Everyone runs up to Burt — 'Great job!' No one cares about me," he says with a grin.

He said he learned so much from Guro Dan. "I respect him not only as a martial artist and teacher, but also for his attitude and philosophy. He is always growing and learning."

Sifu's cup was low so I asked him if he wanted more tea. He said yes and tapped his index and middle fingers on the table, a Chinese custom. He bowed his head and thanked me.

"Reality," he said, "I'm not looking for students. Students will copy what others do. Then they never really get it because they are trying to be someone else. I want leaders. Leaders bring their own ideas and will evolve the art."

"A musket is a traditional weapon. It doesn't mean it's the best one."
Guro Dan Inosanto

Sifu and Burt Reynolds 1980

51

LESSON 12
BUY THEM A PRESENT

If a Sifu says they never get hit, don't believe them.
The more you try, the more you get hit.
When someone hits you, don't get mad.
Instead, you better thank them.
They are your best teachers.
Not the ones that sweet talk you and tell you how great you are.
The people that point out your mistakes are the ones who help you the most.
You better buy them a present.

After an hour and a half, all the food was gone and the dishes were cleared. People were sipping tea, eating orange slices, and exchanging fortunes from fortune cookies. None of us wanted this time to end.

One of the students asked Sifu about separating the role of a teacher and friend with students.

"You can be friends with your students outside of class," he said looking at everyone gathered. "Go out to eat. Have fun. It's great. I used to have my students over to my house all the time in the beginning. I'm not married then, live by myself. I used to make chicken wings all the time. All my students love them.

"But you have to run your school like a business. In the beginning, I'm not doing that. I didn't even charge. Just tell people, 'Pay me what you want.' The honor system. Some people don't pay nothing," he said, laughing.

"I didn't make enough money, so I had a job as a waiter. One day, my students came in and asked for me as their waiter. I felt embarrassed for myself," he said, looking down. "Not because I was serving them — I made chicken wings all the time — but because I realized then my job was to be a Sifu, not a waiter."

Many in the group nodded their heads, probably finding it hard to believe that such a gifted teacher once had to work as a waiter to support himself.

"But you learn," he said.

He was reliving those days as he spoke.

"Fred Degerberg came to my school one time. I had around 70 students, 2,000 square feet. Guro Dan was there."

At the time Fred, who was based out of Chicago, ran the most financially successful martial arts schools in the US with over 70 schools and more than 10,000 students.

"Fred walks in the school, looks around. He says, 'You're pretty good teaching. Guro Dan too. But you're lousy at business. You're terrible.'

"It was true. I didn't get mad. He helped me realize I had to change my mindset around business."

One thing he learned was that he really doesn't like to talk about money. "Now, if someone tells me they can't pay, I tell them to see the office manager. He don't care. He makes them pay," he said laughing. "I learned he is better than me at that."

He went on to stress the importance of learning the difference between what works in a classroom and what works on the street.

"One guy, not my student, was a grand champion in weapons forms. Incredible what he could do. Amazing. Then one day he got mugged coming out of a grocery store. One guy in front, one guy behind. They cut him up, all over his hands. He didn't put the groceries down. Then he realized it's different. Guys who have no training can kill you. You have to be aware. Don't just limit yourself to training in a certain way.

"That's why I don't really shop. Just buy something and put it in my pocket," he said, stuffing his hand into his front pants pocket. "That's it," he said laughing, breaking the tension a bit.

"Sifus get hit more than anybody. If you hear a Sifu say they never get hit, don't believe them. The more you try, the more you get hit. When someone hits you, don't get mad. Instead, you better thank them. They are your best teachers. Not the ones that sweet talk you and tell you how great you are. The people that point out your mistakes are the ones who help you the most. You better buy them a present," he said.

He reiterated his point.

"Thank them and really feel grateful."

The group nodded in understanding.

"After every situation, ask yourself, what did I learn? Learning is more important than winning. If you won and you didn't learn, you won't improve. Then, next time maybe you won't be so lucky. But if every time you learn, and act upon it, then you will always get better. Always ask yourself that question, what did I learn from this? How can I use this to help myself and other people in the future?"

It didn't seem like he wanted the evening to end either. He genuinely relished teaching us.

"In your life there will be a lot of situations that are new to you, that you won't have experience dealing with. Don't worry, go slow. Focus on what you can do. Ask for help. Watch other people. Don't think you have to know everything. The only way you get better is practice, and when you do, you are going to make a lot of mistakes. That's the only way to improve."

Kevin Seaman glanced down at his watch then looked over to Sifu and nodded, "Okay Sir?" We had been there for more than two hours.

"Yes, let's go," Sifu said as he stood up.

We all got up and said goodnight to Sifu and each other. Sifu hugged everyone.

I inhaled the crisp autumn air as I walked out of the restaurant toward my car, realizing that I had a lot of presents to buy.

"Sifus get hit more than anybody."

Francis Fong

LESSON 13
USE YOUR IMAGINATION

There is a saying in Wing Chun:
Legs like a mountain, body like bean curd, head like a crystal.
Train your legs to sink.
Like seaweed, stick to the ground, nothing can move you.
Your body is relaxed, like seaweed flowing in the water.
Your mind is clear.
Visualize what you are doing.
Use your imagination.

I was attacked as I got out of my car.

First by the heat, next by the humidity, and third by pollen so thick it blanketed all of the nearby parked cars with a light green mist. *You've got to be kidding*, I thought, rubbing my eyes, sweat beading up on my forehead in the few moments' walk from my rental car to the Francis Fong Martial Arts Academy. It was July in Atlanta, after all.

For the first couple of years I only trained with Sifu twice a year at seminars held in upstate New York. It wasn't long before I wanted more and began attending seminars within a day's drive.

In May of 1994 I sold my Tony Robbins franchise to a woman who worked for me in the business. Although I learned a tremendous amount from Tony and hold he and his concepts in high regard, as a franchisee I was only able to sell and teach a few programs to a restricted market. Personal coaching, which would have been a natural product progression, was five or six years in the future at that point, so with what I perceived to be limited support for the franchise network, I sold it and moved on.

I started a sales and marketing consulting business and soon acquired Kodak as one of my clients. I designed sales training for their strategic account executives, teams who worked with large customers which purchased products and services from multiple divisions, companies like Disney and Wal-Mart. Kodak liked my work and offered me a permanent position which took me down to their US headquarters in Atlanta once a month. As their Atlanta office was less than 15 minutes from Sifu's Academy in Duluth, I began to attend classes and take private lessons as often as I could. It was through these private lessons that I learned the most.

In July of 1998 I had my first private lesson.

Entering the academy was a respite from the broiling heat outside. A bell clanged as the door shut, capturing the cool fresh air inside. A pair of brown leather high backed chairs were angled symmetrically around a small, ornate table inlaid with mother of pearl Chinese designs to the left of the entrance. Nearby a higher matching table held incense. Above, parchments adorned with Chinese calligraphy hung on either side of a painting of Sifu wielding two butterfly swords crouching low in a cat stance. Across from the painting was a colorful mural of three ancient Chinese warriors.

Dozens of photographs of his students, including a Navy SEAL, NFL players, and a few actors, lined the pale yellow walls. Adjacent were pictures of Ajarn Chai Sirisute and Guro Dan Inosanto, teachers who had been at the Northeast Camp back in 1991 who I'd trained with since. Also hanging on the wall were numerous plaques of accommodations and accreditations from various military and law enforcement organizations, including the Fort Benning Rangers. Each picture and plaque had been signed with heartfelt expressions of gratitude.

Already dressed in my uniform I went directly to the workout area and bowed in. The walnut colored hardwood floor reflected the sunlight and gave slightly under my weight as I walked to the center. Along one side of the room were five wooden dummies set at various levels to accommodate the height of different students. Next to the dummies were a series of poles, each about nine feet long, called Luk Dim Boon Kwan or Six-and-a-Half Point Poles because there were six and a half movements. I wasn't quite sure how you get a half a movement but the Forbidden City in Beijing has 9,999 ½ rooms so I guessed that it was a Chinese thing.

There was a boxing ring in the corner along with four heavy bags – two standard 60 pound boxing bags and two for training Muay Thai – a six foot bag hanging just inches off the floor to develop low, mid and high kicks, and a bag that resembled an onion for training knees and elbows as devastating weapons.

After a few minutes Sifu came in dressed in black wrestling shoes, a black short sleeved top with the Academy logo, and a pair of long black polyester warm up pants which he wore so that, I found out many years later, the hair from his two German Shepherds didn't stick to it.

"Jim, how you doing?" he bellowed from the depth of his diaphragm as he bowed at the entrance of the training room and walked over.

"Great Sifu," I said. I bowed and extended my hand to shake. He took it and embraced me.

"Good to see you," he said smiling. He asked how my trip was and how work was going. After a few minutes of small talk, he asked, "What do you want to focus on today?"

I was surprised by the question. He told me later that he'd always focus on what his student wanted, at least in the beginning. "You are more open that way."

I asked him what he thought I needed to work on.

He nodded. "Let me see your first form."

Siu Nim Tao is the name of first pattern of movements, or form, in Wing Chun Kung Fu. Siu Nim Tao means *the little idea*. It contains important foundational principles and techniques and is the basis for any additional training. "If you don't get the little idea, you won't get the big one," Sifu said. "It's about establishing your center, up, down, sideways, this way, that way, in one situation, in another situation. In Siu Nim Tao you learn proper distance and position, and focusing on your stance."

I demonstrated the movements. He adjusted, tested, guided, and encouraged all along the way. He told me to keep working at it.

"Do I breathe out when extending my tan sao and fook sao, and breathe in when doing wu sao?" I asked, referring to various hand positions in the first section of the form.

He shook his head. "Don't think breathe in, breathe out because you won't be natural. You're analyzing, thinking too much. You can't think. You need to have no mind."

How do I have no mind? I wondered.

"Practice your first form every day. Siu Nim Tao is all about mind-set training. Second form is about your body. Third form is about your spirit, uniting your body and mind."

He started at attention — *Lop Jing* — his feet together and hands at his sides. He seemed to melt into the floor as he bent his knees slightly and sank his weight down. His arms floated up level with his shoulders, and his wrists hung loosely in front, as if connected to small orbs. He smoothly pulled his fists back level with but behind his upper chest, an inch away from his body, to complete the ready position or *Jun Bay*.

He pivoted on his heels and opened up his feet as wide as they could go so that they were 180 degrees from each other, like first position in ballet. He then pivoted again, this time on the balls of his feet, and swung his heels out so that both were at roughly 30 degree angles, pointing inwards in the *Yee Jee Keem Yeung Ma* position, or *Number two goat pinning stance*, so called because your legs look like the Chinese characters for the number two, and because it was the same stance you would use to pin a goat. Most people call it *Keem Yeung Ma* for short.

He pressed his upper back out like a cat and pulled up on his low diaphragm and inner thighs, making him at once solid and rooted at his base, and fluid and relaxed throughout his upper body. He completed the opening section by extending his arms out in a crossed double *gan sao*, and then, keeping his elbows stationary, lifting up to a crossed double *tan sao* position for the opening stance — *Hoi Sick*. He pulled both arms back into fists by his upper chest, close but not touching, then executed a sun punch — *yut jee kuen* — with his left arm, pulled that back, and did the same on the other side.

Each movement was effortless and flowing as if he were performing under water.

He extended his left arm in a tan sao position.

"First form, you need to visualize. Put a candle up at the level of your third eye," he said, touching the point between his eyebrows with the tip of his middle finger. "Try to draw in the candle with your mind as you move in," he said, bringing in his protective hand — *wu sao*, "and push it out as you extend" he added, extending his *fook sao* — sensing hand.

Could he really move the flame with his mind?

Perhaps sensing my question, he said, "Don't worry if you can move the flame or not. Just focus on it. Then, over time," he said, stepping back three paces, "move back further and further from the candle."

He probably could.

He raised one leg up high and balanced on the other, keeping the sole of his foot on the center line, an imaginary line running down the middle of the full length of the body. "Do your form once on one leg, then switch and do another time with the other leg. Over time bring your leg higher and higher until you can do the form with your foot at the level of your solar plexus." He demonstrated.

I raised my left leg up and began the form. I wobbled a number of times and had to drop my foot to the ground twice.

Crap!

He encouraged me to keep working at it, to imagine that my supporting leg was like a sandbag filling up with sand, getting gradually more full and heavy, merging with the ground.

"There is a saying in Wing Chun — Legs like a mountain, body like bean curd, head like a crystal. Train your legs to sink. Like seaweed, stick to the ground, nothing can move you. Your body is relaxed, like seaweed flowing in the water. Your mind is clear and balanced, no thinking. Visualize what you are doing. Use your imagination."

I continued practicing as he spoke.

"Use your imagination. When you extend your tan sao, think of a parachute attached to your arm."

Later in the form he suggested, "When you do moot sao," referring to a downward movement of the arm, "imagine a waterfall. Visualize what you are doing," he repeated. "Use your imagination. Otherwise you are just moving your arms around."

"Where your mind goes, the qi will follow."

Mencius

Sifu Fong with Fort Benning Army Rangers

LESSON 14
DON'T CHASE, DON'T BE GREEDY —
KEEP TO YOUR CENTER

You have to understand your center.
You have to go back there.
Move from there.
Live from there.
Don't chase, and don't be greedy.
Keep to your center.
Your center is not just physical.
You have to understand what it means for your life.

I continued practicing the first form, visualizing as he had instructed. We progressed to a number of drills associated with the movements contained in the form. My energy was much better after visualizing — stronger, yet more relaxed.

After a while, though, I felt myself rushing one of the drills.

"Don't rush," Sifu said. "It takes a long time to execute properly. If you are trying to rush, then you'll miss the important points," he said as we took a break. "Most people want to hit right away. They want to feel strong and confident, so they want to punch something. If you don't teach them that, they will get bored, and they quit.

"But for my private students, I tell them not to worry about hitting too much at first, because if you want to punch, then you are only thinking about that one punch. You will be tense, concentrate only on your fist. You'll forget about your body positioning and sinking your weight down and focusing on your center.

"Your power comes from your position and your entire body, from sinking, not from your arm. I teach my students to focus on the position, and relax your mind. Don't think about hitting. When you are

61

in the right position with your mind relaxed then your punch will be powerful."

I nodded. "So I don't need to go crazy," I said.

"No bonzai," he laughed. "Bonzai is just one way. No return. If someone asks you to go on a trip and they only give you a one-way ticket, better not go, I tell you."

We practiced for a bit more, and then he asked if I was hungry.

I glanced at the clock. It was 11:45. My one-hour private lesson had gone on for almost two.

It would continue through lunch.

We took his car and drove to a restaurant in a nearby mall. It was a chain that he said served good salmon.

After being seated, we quickly looked over our menus and gave the waitress our orders. We both asked for tea, which she brought promptly. As we drank, he asked, "What's important about your center?"

I answered that it provides a reference point, a place to always return to and focus on. From there you can move correctly, gauge where you are at any time, and know how far you should go.

"Exactly," he said.

He then asked me where my center was.

I wasn't sure of the intent of his question, whether he meant center line or center of gravity. I pointed to the area below my navel, known as the dan tian in Chinese.

He smiled. "You have to understand your center. You have to go back there. Move from there. Live from there. Your center is not just physical. You have to understand what it means for your life."

"You mean my priorities?"

"Yes. Your priorities, your values, what's most important to you in life. Siu Nim Tao is very precise. Your elbow is a certain distance from your body. Your hands are in a certain position relative to your body. Your mind has to focus in a certain way."

Having just practiced that for almost two hours, I gained a whole new degree of understanding — being off by just a fraction of an inch or placing my focus on the wrong area meant the difference between astonishing strength and weakness.

"It's simple to do in the form, right?" he asked.

Simpler, I thought.

"You are just by yourself, nobody else. But when you start to drill, then you can lose that positioning, that center. Why?"

I considered his question. "You over-commit. You try too hard. You focus on chasing hands instead of keeping to the center."

He smiled again. "Exactly. When you start to apply it in fighting, it's even harder to stay in position. It's simple but it's not easy. A lot of people can do the form, and even a drill, but it doesn't mean they can apply the technique in a real situation. That's why training needs to be three phases."

I agreed that there was a big difference between the three. "Form, drill, application — FDA," I said. "You have to do all three."

Sifu Fong laughed. "FDA, Form. Drill. Application. That's good."

He was quiet for a while before speaking again.

"It's interesting, you have a form, but you have to apply it. You have a goal, but you need to be flexible. If you're too goal oriented, you're always thinking and analyzing. Then you can't be natural.

"In life it's easy to get caught up in being busy, in the application. It's easy to lose your center, your focus on what's really important."

"Your values, your priorities," I said.

"Exactly. You get greedy. You go after things that really aren't important. You end up chasing," he said. "Always come back to your center, your values. You have to focus on them, make them a priority.. Otherwise you lose what's important. You lose where you are."

I couldn't be sure but it seemed like he was speaking as much to himself as me. We moved on to other topics of conversation, and after a bit I asked him if he still practiced his forms.

He nodded. "I do, but not always the same way. I might focus on a certain part of it. If you just go through the whole form just to do it, like you are checking it off on a to-do list, that's no good."

I am totally a "check it off the list guy". Sometimes I'll even add something to my list that I've already done, just to have the satisfaction of checking it off. Nothing wrong with that, is there? (Note to self – check off that I asked if there is anything wrong with that).

Damn. Must...pay...attention.

"You can do your form 20, 30 years. Who cares?" he said, flailing his arms.

A couple at the next table looked over.

"You have to put feeling into it. You have to learn, test, connect, and check," he added, his hands flowing with a sense of effortless and grace that would take me years to mimic.

I realized that his advice applied far beyond the forms. I was very task oriented in most areas in my life, and come hell or high water, I was going to accomplish my goals. There was upside to that, primarily in the accomplishment of objectives.

The downside was that for some reason, I never felt like I could slow down and savor the present moment. I wasn't sure where in the future I was heading that was going to be so much better than the present, but I was overwhelmingly focused on it. I never quite figured out that the future was going to simply be another present moment.

Being present was, for me, incredibly difficult.

I noted, ironically, that I was halfway through my lunch of salmon, broccoli and rice and didn't remember tasting any of it.

"So, don't just do it to do it," I commented, those few words not even coming close to conveying how much of a challenge that presented.

"Exactly," he answered. "It's so easy to get off center. You get busy. You get into a routine. You forget what is important. In Wing Chun, you need to go back to the form every day to make sure you are starting from the right place," Sifu said.

"Use your art to help your life," I said reflectively, more to myself than to him.

He nodded and we both finished our lunches chatting about other topics. The waitress came and cleared our plates, and asked if we wanted anything else. We both said no and she said she'd be right back with the check.

"Different people like different things to remind themselves of what is important," Sifu said while we waited. "Some people like to pray. Some people like to meditate. Some people like to read. The main thing," he said, "is to consider correct form. Form for behaving, form for living, form for treating other people. If you don't go back to your form, your center, your values, then it is easy to get way off track."

"And the worst part is you probably don't even realize it until it's too late," I added, hoping that it wasn't true for me.

To what extent was I living by my values? I wondered.

Sifu agreed. "Little by little, you get off. That's why you have to test it out, to apply it, see if it works in real situations, in your life. Then, go back to the form, to your values and to the principles that guide your life, and make adjustments to get you back there."

"It's a never ending process," I said.

"Until you die," Sifu smiled. "Then you can stop."

*"Happiness is when what you think, what you say,
and what you do are in harmony."*

Mahatma Gandhi

LESSON 15
STAY WITH WHAT COMES

There is a saying in Wing Chun:
Stay with what comes,
Follow as it retreats,
Thrust forward as the hand is freed.
Don't do before, don't do after, you must move at the same time.
To accomplish this, you can't be ahead, you can't be behind.
Don't think about what happened before.
Don't try to predict what will happen next.
Connect, just let it happen.
Then respond, don't react.
Reaction can be wrong, you can make mistakes.
Train yourself so that you respond correctly.
Just be in the present moment.

"Ahh — wait. Take your time," Sifu said.

I was rushing, trying to anticipate his action during a trapping drill during another private lesson at his Academy.

"Don't do before I do, don't do after I do. You need to move at the same time. You can't stop and think, you can't be analyzing the situation. Don't rush, don't think. Feel," he stressed.

I took a deep breath and exhaled forcefully. "Yes sir. I guess I'm not relaxed."

"You aren't relaxed because you are thinking, analyzing," he noted.

I was good at analyzing. It's a lot of what I did at work. But it wasn't helping me so much here.

"Don't commit."

Okay.

"Let him commit."

66

That would mean I'd have to wait and be patient. Not my strong suit. There seems to be a theme here.

"Don't trap. Let him trap himself. Makes sense to you?"

"Yes, sir" I said, nodding my head.

It makes total sense, I just can't do it.

Yet.

"Don't think about what happened before. Don't try to predict what will happen next. Connect, just let it happen. Then respond. Respond, don't react. Reaction can be wrong, you can make mistakes. Train yourself so that you respond correctly. Just be in the present moment."

There's that present moment again, which was, apparently, my nemesis.

I tried it once more.

The effect wasn't any better.

Thankfully, Sifu suggested we take a break. After about ten minutes we resumed with a different exercise called chi-sao, or sticking hands.

"Whatever I do, just stick to me," Sifu instructed.

I placed my left hand in a fook sao on his right tan sao, and he placed his left fook sao on my right hand bong sao. I did my best to stick to him no matter what he did.

My best wasn't very good. In a matter of seconds I overcommitted and was caught off balance.

He laughed.

I'm glad one of us thinks this is funny.

"Now, Jim. This time don't try to follow me. Just stay to your center, and respond naturally. Don't force it."

He started again. I let go and just responded, abandoning any thought of controlling or anticipating his movements.

I did a little bit better, for about 30 seconds.

"Good," he encouraged. "Better. Now, how about this?" Instead of remaining stationary with his feet planted, he pushed forward.

I staggered backwards from the force.

He grinned.

I didn't.

"I have to work on my grounding," I said.

He shook his head. "You are trying to fight me."

I thought that was kind of the point.
"Don't fight."
Umm.
"Accept. Stay with what comes. Your partner is like the road and you are the car. Go with what comes to you, right away, with no thinking or hesitating. Does that make sense?"

I answered yes, but in truth I wasn't entirely sure. He must have sensed the hesitation in my voice.

"You have to keep centered yourself. If you try to react to your partner, you will always lose. You over-extend, you anticipate, you are reacting."

Now it made sense.

"Like dancing. You have to sense. Don't think or you'll step on my feet."

He extended his left hand. I met his with my left, the back of our wrists touching, and he started a pulling hand drill called lop-lop. Within less than a minute I was overextending.

"Don't reach on lop sao. Bring him to you. Don't go to his place. Like you say you are going to fight, have him come to you. You know your territory. Don't go to him. That's why fighting in other countries on the ground is so tough. They know their territory, other people don't."

We continued the drill, and I sank down into my stance even more.

"Yeah, better," he said, encouragingly. "Bring me to you. Don't over-extend, don't try so hard. Stay with me."

"Yes sir," I answered, my body struggling to do what I intellectually understood. "Do you do what you want or do you react to him?" I asked.

"Both," he said as he continued the drill, frequently changing hands by pushing my elbow.

"You set your mind on what you want and then respond."

That also made sense.

"You see kids playing football and they run backwards to avoid getting tackled. Most times they get tackled anyway, for a huge loss. Do that in the pros and they'll beat the hell out of you in the showers. Everybody pissed off at you," he said with a smirk.

"The same thing is true in Wing Chun. Once you advance and gain ground, don't go back. Elbows never go back."

There are four ranges in martial arts — kicking, punching, trapping and grappling. His point was that once your close the gap between yourself and your opponent and get into close range, don't retreat. Keep that forward energy all the time.

"Go from the 50-yard line, to the 25, to the goal line for a touchdown. Know where you are going then be flexible, like a good runner. Stay with what comes."

We trained for a bit longer then Sifu said, "Okay Jim. How is it? How you feel?"

I glanced at the clock. Again it was past the scheduled two hours. Time just flew. I thanked him for everything, quickly changed in the dressing room and drove back to Hartsfield Airport. I had been in Atlanta for five days and was eager to get home and see my family.

The two hour flight from Atlanta to Rochester was fine, but the trip from the airport home, normally a 15 minute drive, took as long as the entire flight. During my visit down south, upstate New York had experienced a freak snowstorm that had dumped 57 inches of snow in less than 36 hours.

The snow beneath the tires of the airport parking shuttle van crunched as we pulled into the parking lot, the sound of snow when it's near the melting point, which meant it was heavy. The driver pulled up to my car, which also had 57 inches of snow on it. Fortunately he had a shovel and helped me get rid of some of the snow so I could at least get to my snowbrush – that earned him a nice fat tip. Even with his help it took me 45 minutes just to clean my car off.

I was tired from the trip and excited to finally see my wife Jessie and the kids. I pulled into the driveway to find Rachel, Dave and Danny playing in a snow fort they had made in the front yard. "Daddy!" they squealed. They ran up to me, the fabric of their snowsuits swishing. I hugged each of them to me and kissed their cold red cheeks.

"It's so great to see you. I missed you so much," I said.

"Can you believe how much it snowed?" Danny asked.

"We had to shovel the driveway while you were gone," Dave said, proud of himself that at the age of eleven he had been the "man of the house" while I was away.

"Wow. That's amazing. It must have been hard. How did you do that?" I asked.

He shrugged. "Just had to do it," he replied simply. "Everybody helped."

I hugged each of them again and touched the pads of our thumbs together, something I started when they were little. "Thanks for doing that. You guys are awesome," I said as my eyes welled up.

"Show me your fort. It looks so cool."

They gave me the grand tour and asked if I would come out and play. "In a bit. Let me go see mommy first."

For some reason, I was anticipating the same greeting from Jessie. "Finally, you're home," she said. It was not a tone of excitement, but rather of relief, as if I was spelling her from her shift.

I hugged her. After a less than satisfactory length, in my opinion, she pulled away. "The kids and I shoveled the driveway out front, but we didn't do the back so we can't get to the garage or the garbage, so you can do that."

Great welcome home, I muttered to myself as I went to change. I could feel myself tensing up and continued to hang on to my resentment as I shoveled. The physical exertion did little to change my mood.

It took me almost three hours to shovel the back. I came inside, showered and climbed the stairs to our bedroom to dress and unpack my suitcase from the trip. Amongst my clothes was my leather bound notebook. I glanced at my notes from my private lesson with Sifu.

Don't fight. Accept.
Stay with what comes.
He is like the road, and you are the car.

Hmmm.

I did fight it.

I didn't accept how she was feeling or think about what it was like to have to deal with that much snow. Plus the fact that the kids didn't have school but she had work, so she had to make sure they were all set. I hadn't thought about that at all. Rather, I was only focused on what I wanted.

I didn't stay with how she responded. I was seeing the issue solely from my perspective.

He is like the road.
My notes needed a capital S before He. *She is like the road.*
You set your mind on what you want and then respond.

In this case, what I wanted was to be more sensitive, patient and loving, though that hadn't really come across had it?

Use your training to help your life.

As a Christmas present to Jessie many years later, I had all our home movies converted from VHS tapes to DVDs. She beamed when she opened the box and was so excited that we absolutely had to start watching them that day. The first few DVDs were when the kids were babies. Rachel and Dave were born twenty months apart and Danny came along two years and two days later.

I was exhausted just watching the three kids run around and play. There was another DVD that showed the kids at swim lessons, each at their own level and learning at their own pace, Danny trying valiantly to keep up with his older brother. *How had she managed to take care of all of their needs every single day?*

It dawned on me that I had absolutely no part in so much of their upbringing, in so much of what made them the incredible people they are. I also never really understood what her life was like taking care of three kids, at one point all under the age of four, all while going back to school to become a nurse. Though she had a Bachelor's degree in English, she hadn't taken any hard sciences and had to take anatomy, physiology, organic chemistry, and statistics in her first year alone. On top of all that she had to figure out how to get the kids to school, arrange for day care when she had classes, get Rachel to dance, and all of them to play dates, and dressed, and fed, and on and on. Somehow she did it all and managed to graduate at the top of her class with a 4.0.

During those early years of owning my own businesses, I routinely worked 90 hours a week, most of those on my feet. I was tired all the time, and more often than I care to admit I was thinking not of how I could help Jessie, but rather about how my needs weren't being met.

While that wasn't me at my best in the early days, I didn't really have an excuse now. I had a job where I didn't work nearly as many hours, nor the weight of having an income that was solely reliant on what I personally sold. Kodak gave me a nice paycheck every other week and provided excellent benefits.

Even though I didn't have the same pressures, I somehow forgot to tell my body and a good portion of my brain about it. I flipped through my notes that went back to 1991:

You are always fighting yourself.

No one can give you what you don't have.

Relax.

Master yourself.

Sink.

I realized I had a long way to go.

> *"Your partner is like the road, and you are the car.*
> *Go with what comes to you, right away, with no thinking or hesitating."*
>
> Sifu Francis Fong

LESSON 16
LET YOUR HEART AND MIND OPEN

Stay with someone in a conversation.
If you go too far ahead, you are not listening.
You are thinking of what you are going to say.
If you are behind, you will miss what the person is saying.
Stay with the person.
Try to be really listening, not commanding.
Let your heart open, let your mind open.
Connect with them.
Your word is my word.

After a two hour private lesson a few months later, we headed out for lunch at a nearby California Baha restaurant. Sifu said that the fish tacos were good, so we both ordered them.

While we were waiting I asked, "So in chi-sao it's really about controlling yourself, then?"

"Yes and no. It's about them, too. It's like a conversation," he said, leaning in and resting his elbows on the table. "Stay with someone in a conversation. If you go too far ahead, you are not listening. You are thinking of what you are going to say. If you are behind, you will miss what the person is saying. Stay with the person. Really listen."

The word listen, with his Hong Kong accent, sounded to me like lesson.

Maybe the lesson was to listen.

"Try to be really listening, not commanding. Sometimes let someone tell you something first. Let your heart open, let your mind open. Connect with them. Your word is my word. My word is your word. Make sense to you?"

Open my mind. Open my heart. Connect.

I agreed, noting that in most conversations people are just waiting for their turn to speak, not really listening to what the other person is

73

saying, much less trying to communicate.

He smiled. "Exactly. Someone's words may be what they really mean or they may not. Be there. Pay attention to the voice. Pay attention to their body language. That will tell you more."

I paused to consider his advice. I knew this stuff. I even taught other people this stuff. But how often did I actually do it? How often did I truly stay with someone in a conversation? Was I really present, open to them, and intent on listening, really listening? *Lessoning?* Or was I merely waiting to jump in with my thoughts or advice?

"Listen with your ear, then let it flow down to your low diaphragm, then answer with your mouth. Work to develop your sensitivity and intuition so that you don't rely on your mind so much. When you analyze, you judge."

Yup.

"You know, the mind can be evil or an angel. It always wants this and that. It judges and criticizes. It will take snapshots of people, a moment in time, and pins them with a label of good or bad.

"But we've all had times when someone could have taken our picture and labeled us as bad, when we know that in our hearts we are good people just having a bad day," Sifu said.

> *"Most people do not listen with the intent to understand;*
> *They listen with the intent to reply."*

During another private lesson in Atlanta we were practicing a drill

Stephen R. Covey, author of *The 7 Habits of Highly Effective People*

LESSON 17
ACCEPT

Don't fight it.
Accept it.
Don't cling and don't try to avoid.
Accept.
Accept doesn't mean not to act or submit.
It means don't judge: good, bad, right, wrong.
I like this. I hate this. I don't care about this.
Don't think about good or bad.

where the objective was to trap the forearm and hit your partner —
pak da.

"A lot of people don't want to drill because to practice properly you
have to let your partner do it," Sifu said.

Partner, meaning cooperation and collaboration, not opponent.

"You have to let him do the repetitions, to practice the movements
over and over. Some people don't want to let someone else go for that
long, or they don't want to get hit. You don't want to get hit so you try
to stop him. Even if you let him do it physically, mentally you will be
fighting him, and you tense up.

"You need to *accept* the hit. This doesn't mean get hurt. Your
partner needs to go lightly. In fact, he doesn't even need to make much
contact in the beginning. Just go through the movements, accept the
hit, and let your partner practice. But in reality you are practicing at the
same time. You make your partner better, you make yourself better."

That was different from how I practiced, even back in my wrestling
days. We would let our training partners do the moves but the atmo-
sphere was still competitive. Every so often fists would start flying,
especially when people were sucking weight and were cranky.

Accept the hit.

"As he is practicing you learn to relax. If you don't, you tense up and try to anticipate his movement, you will always be thinking instead of feeling. Let him go, learn to relax. From relaxation you will develop a sense of timing. You will begin to sense openings and opportunities." The relaxation Sifu was talking about was so different from my definition. I had to figure out what he was doing.

We continued drilling for a bit, me doing my best to relax. After a while we took a break. "Any questions, Jim, just ask."

It was never about time to him. It was always about teaching his students and I appreciated the opportunity more than he would ever know.

"About accepting — intellectually I get the concept but," I stopped, struggling to put it into words, "How do I get every other part of me to understand?"

Sifu nodded knowingly. "Start your training with a sense of flowing and accepting. This is more your spirit. Open up. Take it in. You can tell if you are open or not. If you aren't, then stop and take a break."

Oddly, I had never considered the option of taking a break.

"Open up, little by little. Realize you aren't accepting. Accept that you aren't accepting."

I laughed. "Accept that I don't accept?"

"Exactly. With each repetition, you notice. You improve. You let go. Little by little, relax your expectations, don't try to control. Don't suppress a thought or feeling. Release it. Guide your thoughts, desires and emotions, don't try to change them forcefully. Accept."

This was *staying with what* comes in practice.

"Then, allow your mind to accept what is happening without judging good or bad, right or wrong. Finally, train your body to complete the movements the right way. That way you start with your spirit open, you progress to your mind, and end with your body movement. Most people start with the physical but never get past it."

I hadn't.

"You have to learn to enjoy the process. If you only enjoy the end result, your joy will be very short lived."

I was finding that out.

"Don't try to control. Just accept things and people the way they are, not the way you think they should be. Little by little, help where you can. Maybe they change, maybe they don't. Just do your best, accept the outcome, accept the process, and accept that you are a certain way too.

"Be like water. It surrounds but doesn't contain. You have to have the mind to do that first, though, otherwise your body won't go along. Don't judge. Don't think about good or bad. As soon as you do you are stopping your mind. You are labeling."

I agreed, in part. "But isn't it natural to judge?"

"Is it?" he asked, raising his eyebrows. "Notice, but don't judge, don't cling and don't try to avoid. Accept. Accept doesn't mean not to act or submit. It means don't judge good, bad, right, wrong. I like this. I hate this. I don't care about this. Make your mind flexible without too much thinking. Be open.

"Once you can learn to be open and accept, then you can control. If you can't accept it, you will always fight it. If you fight, then you can never hope to control anything, especially yourself."

Good point.

Accept and redirect.

"Remember form, drill, application? FDA. You made it up."

"Sure."

"Well, form and drill is there for a reason. Would you buy something that said, "F approved? You wouldn't even know what it was. What's F? You need FDA approved, right? When you have trouble, always go back to the center. Go back to the form. Your values. Your priorities."

"That makes sense," I said.

He remained quiet for a while. I could tell he was thinking deeply about this idea.

"Learn to come back to the center. It's a point of not judging about right or wrong. Who is to say what is right and what is wrong? Just keep practicing. Don't worry about right or wrong. Be open to everything.

"For example, we do a wrong way bong sao, but sometimes the wrong way is the right way, it depends on the situation. Sometimes what you think is good turns out to be bad and what you thought was bad turns out to be good. Be open to anything, don't reject anything. See what the effect is, there is always cause and effect."

He paused, looking down, again deep in thought. After a time he spoke.

"You also have to accept yourself."

I asked him what he meant by that.

"You have to be honest with yourself. If you try to hide a fault and act like you don't have it, you are only kidding yourself. Really, I don't think we change who we are that much in life. You can improve but you don't really change who you are and how you act that much.

"Stay with what comes. It's a testing of your mind and body. Do you fight what comes, or can you accept it? Whatever it is, can you do it? What you get, you get. What you don't get, you don't get. Why get upset about what you don't have? Staying with what comes means accepting the situation, physically, mentally, emotionally and spiritually."

"The way is not difficult, only there must be no wanting or not wanting."

There are 15 levels of Instructor in the Francis Fong Instructor
Chao-Chou

LESSON 18
TEACH FROM THE HEART

You have to decide why you want to teach.
It can't be for your ego.
It has to be to help other people.
I'm a teacher.
It doesn't matter whether I get paid $1,000 or nothing,
I will teach the same way.
Teaching has to come from the heart.

Association (FFIA): five levels of Apprentice Instructor, five levels of Associate Instructor, and five levels of Full Instructor. Each level takes at least one year to complete.

Through the instructor training, I gained insight into how to develop as a teacher. Since I had a lot of experience in the field of training and development and had owned a training company for years — I figured I pretty much had the concepts about teaching down.

I soon discovered that I had a lot to learn.

"As an instructor you have more of a responsibility," Sifu advised when he first began training me as a teacher. "This isn't just about you and your development any more. It's about helping others. I'm not giving you this information just for you to hold on to. You have to share it with others."

"Yes sir," I replied, taking his message seriously.

"Always learning, I tell you. Three things to do well - your own skill, your teaching and your business. If you are good yourself, but can't teach, it's not gonna work. If you have good skills, and are a good teacher but don't have a good business, you can't last. You need to have all three. I don't just look at the person as an instructor. I look at the whole organization. What is your staff like? What is your facility like?

"Also in the classroom, you have three jobs. One job is to teach. You have to show them what to do."

I nodded in agreement.

"One job is to coach. They already know the techniques but you help them do what they already know. Maybe better or more consistently. Point out what they are doing right, what they are doing wrong.

"Third is to guide. You already taught them and you coach them, but guiding is different. Guiding is getting them to explore for themselves.

"Lastly, you have to decide why you want to teach. It can't be for your ego. It has to be to help other people. I'm a teacher. It doesn't matter whether I get paid $1,000 or nothing, I will teach the same way. Teaching has to come from the heart."

> *"The best teachers are those who tell you where to look,*
> *But don't tell you what to see."*

Chinese proverb

Sifu Fong with Kevin Lee at the FFIA Camp

LESSON 19
PLANT SEEDS

A teacher isn't about a length of time.
Like a friend, a teacher can be with you for a long time,
Or only for a moment in time.
One meeting could be it.
Either way, they are no less a teacher, no less a friend.
For most people, your job is to simply give them a seed.
A seed is potential. It's up to them to water it, nourish it, take care of it.
Give for as long as you have with them, then let them go.
Just plant seeds.

In 2000, I began bringing Sifu up to Rochester annually for seminars. My longtime friend Matt Dorsey always supported me in this endeavor and co-sponsored these events. My own students would be there, along with students from upstate NY, New York City and Canada.

While driving him to his hotel in 2001, Sifu asked me about Esther, one of the students he had seen the last time he came to Rochester.

"She left," I answered. "I was sorry to see her go. She was making really good progress. She was with me for about a year, but then," I shrugged, letting my body complete the sentence. "I don't know. She was going back to school to get her Masters in electrical engineering. I'm not sure what happened."

Sifu nodded understandingly. "Jim, a teacher isn't about a length of time. Like a friend, a teacher can be with you for a long time, or for only a moment in time. One meeting could be it. Either way, they are no less a teacher, no less a friend."

"I guess," I said, still feeling a sense of disappointment.

"If a student comes, that is fine. If they leave, that is fine, too. I don't try to get a student to come and I don't try to keep a student from going. If they want to come, they should come. If they want to go, they should go."

He made it sound so easy.

"Stay with what comes, huh, Sifu?"

He smiled. "I know how you feel. You want to help everyone. Be aware of your expectations for others. You can't want it for them. Just guide them and help them discover what they want and need. Make sure you are teaching for them, not for your own ego. Be there for them, to teach and guide them. For what they want, otherwise no one will ever live up to your expectations."

I agreed. Maybe I was too invested in them.

"Think about your children. You have to guide them and take care of them, and you need to set boundaries. But you can't control what they like, what they don't like, what they are interested in or where their passions lie. You can only plant the seeds and nurture them.

"For most people, your job is simply to give them a seed. A seed is potential. It's up to them to water it, nourish it, and take care of it. By the way, you don't know what that seed will develop into. That is up to them.

"For others, you can help to nurture their development and guide them. It's not the same for everyone. You can't help everyone to nurture it. But you can always give people a seed."

I had a chance to see Sifu practice what he preached later that year in Atlanta. I arrived at his Academy thirty minutes before my private lesson, changed, then headed back to the training area. While I was warming up, the senior student entered. I didn't know him well, but I did know that he had moved from up north to Atlanta some years before specifically to train with Sifu. He was an excellent practitioner.

He looked quickly around the school, grabbed a pair of focus mitts, and left. He saw me, but didn't say hello. Not that he knew who I was, but all of Sifu's Academy students whom I had met before were very polite and friendly, and the instructors even more so. I also wondered why he didn't stop in to say hi to Sifu either.

I soon discovered why.

He wanted to go more "hard core". He was no longer satisfied with how Sifu was running the school and wanted to do things his own way. He not only left, but also took a number of students with him.

Sifu came out of his office, said good morning to me, and went out to the parking lot to talk with the guy who, up until that point, had been his senior student.

A few minutes later he came back in and told me the story.

"Wow. That's surprising," I said. Surprising that the guy would leave and surprising that Sifu wasn't mad, especially since he took other students with him. "Aren't you upset?" I asked.

He laughed. "I remember a story Guro Dan told me. One of his senior students left and started his own school. His mother told him, 'Dan, even Jesus had Judas, and believe me, you're no Jesus.'"

He shrugged and grinned. "What can you do? Just plant the seeds. Do your best to help others. How can you know what is best for them? Give for as long as you have with them, then let them go."

*"Don't judge each day by the harvest you reap
but by the seeds that you plant."*

Robert Louis Stevenson

LESSON 20
LOOK BUT DON'T SEE

Look without seeing,
Hear without listening.
Look but don't get hooked.
Don't get caught up too much in one thing,
Otherwise you will over-commit.
You'll get caught.

My job changed, which meant my plane fare to Atlanta was no longer compliments of the company. Luckily there was a weekend seminar in Somerset, New Jersey coming up, which was only a six-hour drive from Rochester.

Sensei Mon Tsang, who studied and taught a few different martial arts, brought Sifu Fong into town twice a year. He had a good turn-out — forty or more people — so he rented out a local Knights of Columbus Lodge for the two days to accommodate the group. All the tables and chairs were pushed away and we trained on the linoleum floor.

Half the guys there were in some branch of law enforcement — easily identified by their close cropped hair, beefy forearms and attentive gazes — their eyes never settling in one place for long.

The other half looked like guys the cops would go after.

After the introduction, Sifu warmed us up with footwork drills, then had us partner for a drill called *pak / sut*. Each person took a right lead stance and advanced with a slapping hand — *pak sao*, followed quickly by a cutting hand — *sut sao*. He had us go back and forth for ten minutes, which was about nine minutes of our deltoids screaming at us to stop. It's amazing how quickly fast repetitive movements can tire you out. Most of the group was circling their arms after just a few minutes, trying to dissipate the burning in their shoulders.

"Can we switch sides?" someone asked.

"Don't switch. Stay same side."

Interesting.

Each seminar was completely different than the others. Sifu said he never went in with any set idea of what he was going to teach. Rather, he sensed the group and what they needed.

The group there was pretty hard core and used to hard physical training, so he started with that. Finally, he let us switch to the other side and ran us through for another five minutes, then called the group to the center.

"Look without seeing. Does that make sense?"

Not yet.

"You need to look, but don't see. Hear, but don't listen. Do you know what I mean?" He looked around the room at the participants, mostly men, a blend of young and older.

"Like a good cop. He'll stop you for speeding and you say, 'Oh, sorry officer. Was I going a little fast? Well, see that's because ...', and you go on and tell them this big, long story. All the while he's writing out a ticket, nodding his head, 'Uh huh ... yep ... sure ... I understand, these things happen.'

"Then he gives you the ticket anyway."

Everyone laughed — half because they had heard that and the other half because they had said it.

"But you think, 'Oh, he's such a nice cop, he listened to me!' But you still get the ticket, right? So be like the cop. Look but don't get hooked. Like the cop, he listens, but it doesn't affect him. If you get caught too much in one thing, if you overreact or over-commit, you'll get caught."

He asked everyone to get in jut sun ma (sideways stance) with our right foot forward.

"Look up," he instructed. "Can you see the floor?"

"No, sir."

"Look down. Can you see the ceiling?"

Again, no.

85

"Look left and you can't see right, look right and you can't see left," he said.

He paused to let that message sink in.

"Now, look at the center."

We did.

"Can you see everything?"

We could.

"Don't get hooked. Keep your gaze soft, in the center. Focus straight ahead but use your peripheral vision too. It's the difference between concentrating," he said, jutting out his neck and staring straight ahead, "and focusing," he added, pulling back his head and relaxing. "When you drive, do you concentrate?" he asked, again staring straight ahead? "Let me know how that goes! No! You focus on driving but are able to see everything around you. Same thing in shooting. In target shooting you can focus on the target because that's all there is. In a real situation," he shook his head quickly. "No way. You have to be aware of the entire area.

"Look but don't get hooked. Focus, don't concentrate."

Sensei Mon had put Sifu up in a nearby hotel. Sifu invited me to share his room with him. As a young man with a wife, three kids and more responsibilities than money, I appreciated the generosity and the opportunity.

We ended up talking late into the night.

His point about not getting hooked was gnawing at me. "How do you not get caught, Sifu? How do you remain detached but not become uncaring?"

He smiled. "That's a good question. My English might be no good. What is the difference between detached and unattached?"

I explained that being detached connoted a sense of aloofness, of being disinterested. Not involved or concerned with. Uncaring.

Unattached, on the other hand, meant not being associated with any particular group, thought or body. It was more about being separate from something else and spoke to relative positioning.

He raised his finger in the air. "That's it. Unattached, not detached. Unattached you still care, but you don't let how you feel stop you from what you need to do. Make sense to you?"

I nodded.

"You don't like to get hit. But you have to remain unattached to the hit. You need to focus on what you want. Long is short, short is long."

"I'm not sure I follow you, Sifu."

"Like setting a goal for yourself, you do what you need to do in the short term for the long term. In the short term, you need to train with lots of people, experience lots of things. Be unattached to how you do. Think about the long term, what you want."

I nodded again. "Okay, that makes sense. So don't be attached to the outcome in the short term, don't care so much. Focus on the long term outcome, on what you want."

"Exactly."

"Don't get hooked. Keep your gaze soft, in the center."

Sifu Francis Fong

LESSON 21
COOPERATE, DON'T COMPETE

Don't compete. Cooperate.
Push each other to get better. That's the best way.
Sometimes you will be better, so teach your partner.
Sometimes others will be better than you,
Hopefully they will share what they know with you.
You are better than someone else? Who cares?
They are better than you? Big deal.
Just try to help everybody, that's the most important thing.

Sifu was explaining a *dan chi-sao* — single hand sticking hands — drill at a seminar in Rochester. A few picked it up quite well, while others struggled. Not surprising, really, as there were practitioners from other Kung Fu styles, Karate, Kali, Muay Thai, and Tae Kwon Do in attendance. Each brought very different backgrounds to the exercise.

"Take your time," he encouraged. "You have to help each other, cooperate with each other. Otherwise, it's not going to work."

A number of people nodded their heads, knowing that they were more competitive than cooperative.

"There used to be all this secrecy in martial arts. No one shared anything with anyone else. If you were a student of one instructor you could never go study with someone else. You would be cut off."

That was, unfortunately, still true today.

"That's no good," he continued, shaking his head. "It's better to be open. Everyone has the same problems. Different languages but we all say the same thing. Just help everyone you can, that way we all get better together.

"Push each other to get better. That's the best way. Everyone should try to help each other get better. Don't compete," he said, smashing his fists together. "Cooperate." He placed his palms together, one inching ahead of the other.

"Help each other."

He spent the next few minutes going around coaching people who were struggling to grasp the drill. He also made sure that myself and the other Wing Chun instructors walked around and helped everyone. After a while he called the group back to the center.

"Sometimes you will be better, so teach your partner. Sometimes others will be better than you, so hopefully they will share what they know with you. You are better than someone else? Who cares? They are better than you? Big deal. Nobody cares, I tell you. Just try to help everybody, that's the most important thing."

He looked around the room. I hoped people were valuing his advice as much as I was.

"Cooperation instead of competition is not just for martial arts. In a conversation, instead of saying, 'No, you are wrong.' Try, 'I see your point. What do you think about this?' Compromise with each other. That way it can work out.

"Three things not to talk about: politics, religion and family matters. Why? Because you can't win. You will lose, lose your friendship. You only have your point of view. If someone says they are a Democrat, I say, 'me too!' If someone says they are a Republican, I say, 'me too!'" he said, laughing.

"What does it matter, really?" he continued, shrugging. "Best way is to work together to make things better. That's all that matters. Not who you are, what you are, it's nothing.

"Respect is most important. It's not about who's better than who or who is afraid of who. It's about helping each other, teaching each other. That's the only way you can get better. You have to help each other.

"Train slowly, not competitively. If you do chi-sao and start slapping each other, you'll only end up getting pissed off, try to kill each other," he said, laughing. "You will never develop the sensitivity and position.

"You help your partner, you are really helping yourself."

"It is one of the beautiful consequences of this life that no man can sincerely try to help another without helping himself."

Ralph Waldo Emerson

Sifu demonstrating relaxed power with Vic Spatola

LESSON 22
LITTLE BY LITTLE, ALMOST THERE

In teaching, don't show them something they can't see.
Don't ask them to feel something they can't feel.
Stay at their level, move the target little by little.
Let them know they are almost there but not quite.
That way they believe they can do it.
Then they keep trying, they keep improving.
In the same way, you have to believe for anything to work.
If you don't believe, it will never work.

In 2000, Sifu Fong began to hold Instructor Training camps in Atlanta. These four-day events were invitation-only seminars held twice a year, and the focus was on the development of the instructors as practitioners and teachers.

Throughout the sessions, he would invite various instructors up to teach the rest of the group a concept. He wanted to test both our knowledge and our ability to teach at the right level. After one of the instructors walked us through a drill, Sifu worked with him on the concept he was teaching.

"Okay, good. Almost there," he encouraged. The instructor continued on, all the while Sifu commented, "Yes. Almost. Good. Better."

After a minute or two he stopped. "Almost got it. Almost. See?" he asked, looking around at the group.

"That is a better way to encourage. Let someone know they are almost there, but not quite. That way they keep trying. They believe they can do it. If they don't believe, it will never work," he said, shaking his head.

"If they believe, then they will keep on trying. If you say, 'No, you don't have it,' their mind will fight that or they will become discouraged.

Instead it is better to keep moving the target. Almost there! They have to believe for it to work.

"My son Nicky brought me a picture of a car he drew," Sifu continued. Nicky was five years old at the time. "I wouldn't look at the scribbled crayon marks all over the page and say, 'That's terrible. What kind of car is this?' Instead, I encourage him. 'That's a great picture!'

"The same is true as you teach. You encourage a person at his or her level. You need to teach at the level that your students can understand. Don't show them something they can't see. Don't ask them to feel something they can't feel. That is called a waste of time. Teach at the appropriate level."

The class continued on practicing various drills for another 10 minutes or so and then Steve Grantham, one of the Sifu's senior students at the Academy, instructed us to get down on the wooden floor for 10 count knuckle push-ups, one of the physical requirements for belt testing. We all made fists and got into the ready position, only our bottom two knuckles — pinkie and ring finger — making contact with the unforgiving hard wood floor.

Really hard wood.

"Down," Sihing Steve commanded.

We dropped down with our bodies resting just above the floor and counted in unison up to 10 in Cantonese: "*Yut, yee, sam, say, um, luk, chut, bak, gow, sup.*"

"Up. One," Steve said. "Down."

The minimum requirement for advanced belts was 25. The pressure on your fists could get to you if you let it. It was a test of your mind as much as your body.

Most people got to 25, and dropped quickly after that.

A few got into the 30s.

When we got to 35 there was only me and one other guy, a young buck from the school, some years my junior. My arms were shaking and the sweat was dripping off my nose and puddling onto the floor but I just kept focusing on the counting, and picturing myself doing one more. I figured no matter how tired I was I could always do one more.

The other guy dropped at 38.

I did 43 when Sihing Steve called it, thankfully (Sihing means more senior Kung Fu brother).

Sifu asked me if I had been practicing those push-ups.

I hadn't, not the full exercise anyway. I had been practicing holding the positions both at the top and bottom portions — those static plank holds were useful in developing core, shoulder and wrist strength — and I had spent a lot of time visualizing.

Another requirement was to do the first form on one leg.

After we all did that on both legs, Sifu had us raise our foot to the level of our solar plexus and hold it in position with our same-side hand.

"Do it for five minutes a day, each side," he said. "But in the beginning, just lift a little bit. Lift up to a box, then, a chair, then a table. Keep going, little by little. If you try to do it all at once and you never did it before, you won't be able to do it. So go slow, but keep going."

He went around helping various instructors. After two minutes, most people had dropped. Once again it was down to me and another young guy, a different one this time, a Yoga practitioner from India who was very flexible and appeared quite comfortable balancing on one leg.

He probably did tree pose for hours, I thought.

I focused on my raised leg and started to wobble, then remembered Sifu's coaching and put my focus on my support leg, balancing out the two sides of my brain. The wobbling stopped.

We both balanced for a bit longer when Sihing? Steve called time, for which I, at least, was thankful.

Sifu smiled. "Everyone, keep practicing."

We continued training for another hour or so. He called everyone to the center. "One thing so important, you should do better than me. Something that might have taken me thirty years to understand, I can teach to you in a few minutes. And your students should be doing better than you, too. If your student knows two moves, then you have to know four. If he knows four, than you have to know eight. Always be ahead but don't show them a hundred moves, they will get overwhelmed and feel discouraged. That's called wasting time.

"Make sure they believe."

A guy takes over as manager of a manufacturing plant. Everything is going along pretty well until one day, six months later, the entire operation comes to a grinding halt. The production line is completely shut down. None of the engineering, maintenance or production crew can figure out what is wrong. After hours of fruitless attempts, the plant manager remembers a business card his predecessor had given him for just such an occasion. "He's expensive," he cautioned, "but worth it."

The manager calls the consultant and asks him to come out as quickly as he can. After a bit the consultant shows up and meets with the manager, who is on the verge of panicking. "No one can work, no orders are being produced or shipped," he almost shouts.

The consultant calmly says, "I'll go take a look." He walks around the production line, peers into a few places, and then makes one tiny adjustment with a screw driver. Instantly the production line starts back up. The plant manager is elated until moments later when the consultant gives him his bill.

"$10,000? For turning a screw?" he asks.

The consultant shakes his head. "No, $1 for turning the screw and $9,999 for knowing which one to turn."

LESSON 23
YOU ARE YOUR BEST TEACHER

You might be with your teacher for an hour or two a day,
But you are with yourself twenty-four hours a day.
You are your best teacher.
A teacher can teach,
But you are taught only when you make it part of yourself.
You have to make it your own.
Trust yourself and your own nature.
You must believe in yourself.

During dinner at a nearby Thai restaurant the second night of the Instructor Camp, Sifu elaborated further on teaching.

"You might be with your teacher for an hour or two a day, but you are with yourself twenty-four hours a day. You are your best teacher."

He took a sip of tea.

"Sometimes people ask me, 'Sifu, should I eat meat or not? Should I become a vegetarian? Should I drink alcohol or not?' I tell them it's up to them. Their body will tell them what is good or not good for them. You have to know yourself. You have to help them understand themselves.

"If you tell your student what to do, then they are dependent upon you. Better to ask them, 'What do you think? Does it make sense to you or not? Yes or no?' That way they have to think for themselves about the situation, not rely on you. You help them but don't do their thinking for them.

"A teacher can teach, but you are taught only when you make it part of yourself. You have to make it your own. Wing Chun is a system, just like boxing, but you develop what works for you in the system. George Forman is a boxer but his style is very different than other

95

fighters because he has made it his own. You make your art your own."

"Everybody approaches it differently," someone said.

"Exactly. What works for me and my body type might not work for you, for your size. You have to make it your own. And everyone learns differently. Right? How many students at your school?" he asked Mark Mills, an instructor from South Carolina.

"About a hundred, sir," he answered.

"And do any two learn the same?"

He shook his head.

"See what I mean? Some people are good at copying others. They see someone else and they can do the technique right away. Others have to do it for themselves, to feel it, then they know. You have to figure out how you learn and understand how your student learns. You'll learn more from the people who are hard to teach. Not the ones who pick everything up quickly.

"To teach is different than a teaching. You can teach but the other person has to assimilate the teaching. Sometimes you need to set up an experience for the other person. You can teach all day long about what an apple tastes like but the only way another person can know it is to taste it him or herself."

He glanced down at his plate. "Like this," he picked up a piece of octopus. "You have to try it to know what it tastes like." He offered it to Adell Dobey, a five term Sheriff from South Carolina who was sitting across from him.

He put his hands up and grinned. "No thanks, Sifu."

Adell is a quiet man. He doesn't say much, but his eyes don't miss a thing. His face is friendly yet alert in a relaxed way, like he believes in the inherent goodness of people, but has also seen the worst.

"Look at a baby. They put something in their mouth that they don't like and their whole body reacts. It's not, 'Oh, how do I feel about this?' Their face scrunches up and they spit it out. Their learning is right there, honest, with their whole body. Right?"

Everybody laughed as he offered the octopus to the Sheriff again.

"It is my responsibility as a teacher to get the information out in a way the student can understand. I have to give him or her the experience so that they can go through it. Then they are learning. It's better than

1,000 words. Nobody can tell you, you have to go through it yourself.

"I have to always change. If the students don't understand, that's my fault. So, it's a challenge to always change what you do as a teacher to guide, to coach different kinds of people. My responsibility is to make sure I can get the information across."

He added that it is the students' responsibility to practice and that as a teacher we had to do the same thing.

"That's why it's hard for me to teach by a curriculum, really. That's not my way. I have to feel the energy of the person or the group, what they are getting or not getting. Then we can flow. From one thing, they get another thing. From this they get that. It's good to have a set teaching curriculum, you need that for a school and that's why we have it for instructors, but more important is energy and an understanding of your students. You have to feel it."

Sifu was exceptional at reading people.

"Don't be in too much of a rush to learn. Take your time, let it come naturally. Don't force it. The same thing with teaching. Don't teach too much at once. Give your student just a little bit at a time. In first form, just teach first section. If they get that, then go to second and then third once they can do the first two. They need to digest it. Like food, you can't stuff their mouth. They need to take small bites, chew and swallow. Otherwise they will choke."

He offered the octopus once more to Adell, kiddingly.

"You don't have to say 'that's wrong.' You don't have to say that's not correct, say improve. Just ask, 'How's this? Which one is better?' They'll know.

"You have to help them learn from their best teacher."

"The teacher opens the door,
But you must enter by yourself."

Chinese proverb

Sifu Fong demonstrating grounding.

LESSON 24
VISUALIZE WHERE YOU WANT TO GO

When you train your mind,
then your body will come along.
When your mind knows what to do,
your body doesn't have to work so hard.
You know people say, "No Sweat"? Why?
Because it's easy, they don't worry.
Train your mind first,
visualize what you want.

One August, I attended a seminar hosted by owners and head instructors Alex Chan and Luigi Cuellar of NuBreed Martial Arts in Queens. I picked up Eric Winfree in Syracuse along the way and he and I made the drive together to New York. We were making good time until we got over the George Washington Bridge. Then we were welcomed to New York by many, many nice cars and trucks, all going in the same direction we were, and what should have taken 15 minutes took over two hours.

Eventually we got to their school, just off exit 35 on the Cross Island Expressway, on 14th Avenue in the village of Whitestone in Queens. Whitestone had a diverse population and what appeared to be a very family oriented, traditional values type of town. The kind of place where people still did business with a shake of the hand, where a person's word was his bond.

We found their school in the middle of an upscale strip mall and parked around back in the garage. As I climbed the stairs I noticed that the windows were professionally adorned with the names of the different arts taught there: Savate – Muay Thai – Wing Chun Kung Fu – Jun Fan Kung Fu / Jeet Kune Do – Brazilian Jiu Jitsu – USA

Boxing – Capoeira – Combat Shoot Wrestling – Filipino Martial Arts.

We walked into what could have been, sans the martial arts theme, the lobby of a five star hotel. Behind the reception area was seated a beautiful woman whose long hair matched the black desk. With a smile that reached her eyes, she shook our hands with a firm grip — it was obvious she trained there. She told us her name was Jessica and helped us register for the event. Eric picked up on her slight accent and discovered that she too was originally from Texas. They spoke about how friendly and chatty people from Texas are compared to people from New York.

They proved their point, chatting for more than 10 minutes.

Being from New York and not quite as chatty, I looked around. To the right was a flat screen TV showing a continuous loop of action shots of students and instructors in the various arts. The main room was covered in dark walnut flooring. Along the right side were five identical wooden dummies, all set to different heights. There was a full length mirror running on the opposite wall, above which, written in big, bold letters, was the saying:

Black Belts are White Belts who never gave up.

To my left was a pro shop featuring NuBreed branded clothing, focus mitts, bag gloves, books, and other equipment.

I walked to the back. Once past the main room, there were a series of wooden cubbies for students to place personal belongings, as well as shoes, as there was a sign *No shoes in the training area*. I took off my sneakers and walked into the back room. To the left was an MMA octagon, the cage made of black mesh. To the right a boxing ring, heavy bags, a speed bag, and a top and bottom bag. Both rooms were entirely covered in thick red and blue protective matting. The space was large — the two rooms combined had to be 80 by 40 feet or more.

Still further back were three more rooms.

The first was a changing room painted a stylish pea green.

The second a break room outfitted with healthy snacks, the walls of which were covered with laminated plaques holding instructor certifications for their students. Each plaque was identical and lined up perfectly on the wall.

The third room was a meditation space which featured a 12 foot square picture of the Buddha on one wall, with candles and meditation benches along the sides.

The attention to detail and the thought put into the physical layout was impressive. That carried over to the attention they gave their students and the expectations and requirements for their instructors, as well. Each instructor had to attend a two year NuBreed University Leadership development program.

I made my way back to the main floor and talked with other students while warming up. After a few minutes Luigi and Alex came in with Sifu Fong. Luigi looked stylish as ever, wearing a long dress shirt, a leather bracelet, jeans, a necklace, and snakeskin cowboy boots with toes so pointy they looked lethal enough to use for his Savate classes. His long black hair was pulled back into a ponytail and his goatee was flecked with grey. He reminded me of Enrique Iglesias.

Alex, on the other hand, reminded me of a military officer. His hair, closely cropped on the sides and tight on top, helped to complete the look. He was wearing warm ups and sneakers, and looked ready to run a marathon.

Or command troops to take a hill.

Or both.

Sifu looked the same as always — relaxed, happy, peaceful, and energetic — he never seemed to age. Eric and I said hello to all three, man hugs all around. We were family.

The seminar got under way and about 30 minutes into the training, Sifu called us into the center of the room. "Try this," he said. "Have your partner push your wrist towards your body in a wrist lock." He reminded everyone to take it easy on their partner, be careful and tap out. He walked around helping people get the technique correctly.

"Okay. Now, by yourself," he instructed, "push your own hand in towards your body, bending your wrist, putting pressure there."

After we did, he asked, "You can push it further, right?"

Everyone agreed.

"Now, have your partner try it again."

Once we did, he asked, "How many people could take more before you tap out?"

Again, everyone agreed.

"You can take more. Why? Because you went further yourself. You are no longer fighting. Your body is used to going further and your mind is used to going further. You have expanded your limits and you relax and let go.

"First train your mind. If you develop your mind, then your body will come along. So when you train your mind, why should you sweat? You know people say, 'No Sweat'? Why? Because it's easy, they don't worry. If you sweat just thinking, then there's something wrong with you. So just train your mind first, visualize what you want, and visualize where you want to go."

"I never hit a shot, not even in practice, without having a very sharp, in-focus picture of it in my head."

Jack Nicklaus

LESSON 25
CONTROL YOUR MIND, CONTROL YOUR BODY

You have to work on your centering.
Once you are centered,
then you can control the mind.
And when you discipline your mind,
you can control your body.
Without control of your mind and body,
you can never master yourself.

"Train your mind to relax. If your mind is on your elbow, then it won't be on your feet. If it is somewhere, then it is not somewhere else. In your stages of development, first you focus on the body. You look at your hand to see if you are correct," Sifu mimed, turning his hand over. "You stare at your feet wondering if the stance is right," he said, looking down. "That's natural. Over time, though, you will develop your mind, focusing it in ways that are more powerful."

The group of us at NuBreed would soon see that.

"Ultimately, though, your mind will not be anywhere.

"Once you are relaxed, your mind knows what to do, so your body doesn't have to work so hard. You can't separate your mind from your body. Mind and body aren't separate. Mind affects body, body affects mind."

Someone asked him what he thought about meditation.

He shrugged. "Meditation is good, it helps relax your mind. But you can meditate anywhere, anytime. There are formal meditations — walking meditations, sitting, postures for your hands, breathing, eyes. You can visualize your feet are like melting butter in a pan as you walk. Walking down the aisle to get married is a meditation. You don't run, unless it's the other way!" he kidded.

"Siu Nim Tao is a meditation, too. Be able to meditate anywhere, at any time. Be able to relax your mind. If you can't relax your mind, your body will never relax."

He went on to describe the power and importance of visualization, of making things so real and vivid. "But it's not just a picture, what you see. It's also about how you feel, your energy.

"If you think about hitting, then your body will tense. If you think about fighting, then you can't relax. You have to work on your centering. Once you are centered, then you can control the mind. And when you discipline your mind, you can control your body. Without control of your mind and body, you can never master yourself."

He asked Alex Chan to come to the center.

"Look here," he said. He sank down in a Kim Young Ma stance, his upper body relaxed. He had Alex extend his left side tan sao. Sifu extended his right hand, his fingertips barely touching Alex's forearm. Sifu didn't physically move his hand back but Alex was drawn forward up onto the balls of his feet. His heels lifted off the ground and he had to step forward to keep from falling.

Sifu then broke what minimal physical contact he had, stepped back two paces and brought his hand back slowly. Once again, Alex fell forward.

The group murmured oohs and ahhs.

"Now, no hand. Just mind." Sifu lowered his eyelids until they were almost completely shut. In a matter of moments, Alex was drawn forward with a force he later described like a powerful magnet.

The room erupted in applause.

Sifu went behind Alex about fifteen feet.

"Now, Sifu Alex can't see me. No mirror, no nothing." Sifu Fong breathed in and drew his hand back. As he did, Alex fell backwards. He moved his hand forward, and Alex again went up on the balls of his feet and stepped forward. When Alex settled, still turned around, Sifu made a circling motion in the direction of Alex's right knee. Within five seconds, Alex's knee buckled.

Everyone clapped again in amazement. Alex smiled, shaking his head.

Sifu smiled too. "Your mind is so powerful. Try it at home."

Usually it was don't try this at home.

"Okay. Look it here," Sifu said, coming back to the center to show another more physical drill. He knew that some people were drawn to the energy work and others weren't, so he didn't want to dwell on it. He had planted the seeds. He did his job showing what was possible.

"Recitations and physically difficult practices,
even if done for a long time,
will bear little fruit if done with a wandering mind."

Shantideva, 14th century monk

LESSON 26
AND 1 AND 2 AND 3...

And one and two and three.
And helps you work on the connection,
the space between the techniques.
Pay attention to the timing, to the connection.
When you practice, do so with a constant flowing
of both the physical movement and your thinking.
Don't just think about the outcome, think about the connection.
But you have to be relaxed. Don't force it.
Like nature, let your practice develop naturally, too.
Otherwise you will always be rushed.

"Get your timing down. You have to do it over and over, and use your training time in the right way."

He called Luigi up to demonstrate.

"With your partner, everyone do this – my side – hit *and* open *and* strike," he said as he executed a series of movements ending in a *wan jern* — side palm strike — that stopped just short of Luigi's face. He had everyone walk through the drill, repeating with him with each of the three movements, "Hit *and* open *and* strike."

After a few repetitions, he asked us to switch.

"Now, when your partner comes to you that is your time to focus."

Our time to focus?

"Get your timing down. Don't just wait until it is your turn."

As Luigi performed the drill, Sifu said with each strike, "I let him come to me. He comes to me. Over and over. I just relax, I get the timing. Once I get the timing, then I can counter," he said as he countered Luigi's palm strike with a blistering strike of his own.

"Or this," he said as he grabbed Luigi's fingers and twisted them into a finger lock, forcing Luigi to immediately tap out.

"Or this," as he chopped and finger-speared Luigi, just grazing his throat, four times in the space of a second.

All Luigi could do was laugh.

"Same thing, when practicing forms, practice in small parts. Do the first section, then the first and second, then first, second and third. Do the first section fifty times, then first and second another fifty times, then do all three fifty times.

"Once you memorize the form, don't just keep doing the whole form. Break it down even further to a series of three movements."

He walked over to the *mook jang*, or wooden dummy.

"On the dummy, do *and* one *and* two *and* three," stressing the word *and*. "Then backwards, three *and* two *and* one, *and* one *and* two *and* three." He demonstrated a sequence of movements, flowing back and forth over the triplet, like a musician playing notes.

"Now your turn," Sifu said.

He had us line up behind the dummies and practice. "One *and* two *and* three," he guided, sounding like a dance teacher, "*And* four *and* five *and* six."

We practiced the sequence of movements over and over, forwards and backwards, Sifu's sing song coaching keeping time. After what must have been thirty repetitions of the full series, the first five of us relinquished our spots for the next group and went back to the end of the line, practicing in the air. We continued in that fashion until everyone had had a turn on the dummy.

Later on we were practicing the *battle punch*, a series of rapid succession chain punches. "Like this," he showed us. "When you hammer in a nail, if you swing the hammer back too far, you will bend the nail. Instead, follow the nail with quick hits, one-two-three. Same thing in hitting, one-two-three," he said, the words in rapid succession.

"But in beginning you pay attention to the timing and the spacing. One *and* two *and* three. Why do you say *and?*" he inquired.

He got various answers.

"And helps you work on the connection. The space between the techniques. Pay attention to that."

The space between the techniques, I repeated to myself.

The pause between the words.
The gap between the actions.
Life between achievements.
Life.
"It's all timing, connection."

After a short break Sifu had us work on Siu Nim Tao, the first form.

"Everybody, relax, let your hands drop to your sides. When you are relaxed you will feel a tingling sensation in your fingertips."

This is often referred to as pulling silk.

"If you lose that sensation you are too tight, too tense. Relax," he guided. "Make that connection. Breathe in," he said, bringing his hand back towards his body in an effortless, graceful manner, hypnotically springing from something or somewhere other than his arm.

"Breathe out," he said, extending his tan sao in the same fluid motion, as if he were under water.

Is that just years of practice I wondered? Just as quickly I dismissed that notion. I knew it wasn't. Many of us around the room had practiced for years, yet hadn't achieved that same effortlessness of movement.

"When you practice forms, do so with a flow. Like dancing, one and two and three and four … there is no break, but a constant flowing to both the physical movement and your thinking. Don't just think about the outcome, think about the connection."

Connection. Connection to what? Was he feeling or sensing something that I wasn't? Was it qi?

"But you have to be relaxed."

Clue number one to feeling the connection.

"Don't force it," he added.

Clue number two.

"Like nature. Let your practice develop naturally, too. Otherwise you will always be rushed."

I had to reorient my training approach to start from a place of relaxation and flowing and build from there. Trying to force it and rely on strength and then trying to relax wasn't getting me too far.

Actually, I had to reorient my life approach to start from a place of relaxation and flowing and build from there.

"The notes I handle no better than many pianists.
But the pauses between the notes — ah, that is where the art resides."

Artur Schnabel

Sifu and Luigi Cuellar at the Francis Fong Martial Arts Academy

LESSON 27
WORK ON YOUR FOUNDATION

Everyone is always concerned about their hands.
If you don't have the foundation, your hands are not gonna be good.
Nobody has good hands and bad footwork.
Working only on your hands and not on your footwork is like
dressing up nice, shirt, tie, hair, everything,
then going out with no pants on.
Practice your footwork.

Sifu had us train for a bit longer then posed a question to the seminar group.

"Why are some movements done three times?"

He showed the first three moves of the second section of the dummy form, three pak sao hands.

"What about Siu Nim Tao?"

He demonstrated the part of the form with three fook sao hands and three wu sao hands.

He asked the same question about Chum Kiu and Bil Jee, the second and third empty hand forms, demonstrating numerous movements and strikes which were each done three times.

He got various responses to his question.

"Because it's important," he said simply. "You like something, you do it more than once." He took an imaginary shot. "Oh, that's good!" He took another, then another. "Something's good, do it three times," he joked.

"Three major hands in Wing Chun, bong sao, tan sao, fook sao. Everybody say bong, tan, fook," he instructed.

"Bong, tan, fook."

"Again."

"Bong, tan, fook."

"Good, your Chinese is good. Better than Hong Kong. I tell you, people don't know the names of the moves. We just do them. You know more than people in Hong Kong."

He walked back over to the dummy.

"Pretty much everything in the dummy form comes from Siu Nim Tao and Chum Kiu. A little from Bil Jee, third form, but mainly first two forms. Siu Nim Tao is your mind, Chum Kiu is your body and Bil Jee is putting them together for your spirit.

"Work on your foundation. Don't just go through the motions. Everyone is always concerned about their hands. If you don't have the foundation, your hands are not gonna be good. Nobody has good hands and bad footwork."

He moved around like a boxer, executing a jab, cross, hook combination in the air, emphasizing his footwork.

"Three things to focus on. Structure. Position. Execution," he said. "I don't even look at someone's hands. I look at their feet, their structure. Get your structure down first. Practice your footwork. Then your position. Only then should you work on execution.

"Working only on your hands and not on your footwork is like dressing up nice, shirt, tie, hair, everything, then going out with no pants on."

"Work on your foundation. Don't just go through the motions."

Sifu Francis Fong

LESSON 28
LEFT SIDE, RIGHT SIDE

The left side of your brain controls the right side of your body.
The right side of your brain controls the left side of your body.
You can't only use one side — you will be off balance.

"Everybody look here please," Sifu said. He was demonstrating the second part of the Siu Nim Tao form to about forty Rochester seminar participants.

"You do double lan sao," he began. *Lan sao* is a bar hand where your forearm is roughly parallel to the ground and level with your shoulders. Double lan sao is putting one forearm on top of the other. "Left hand on top. Got it?" he asked.

He demonstrated the next movement, double *sut sao* — throat killing hand strikes out to the sides, and the next, coming back into a throat-tightening hand — *saut gan sao*.

"Now, which hand on top? Right or left?"

"Right," those who knew the form answered.

"Why?"

Some of us knew but wanted to let others learn from him.

Sifu asked me to come up. I ran up and saluted by placing my left hand over my closed right fist as a sign of respect, something everyone was expected to do with their partner before each drill. He asked everyone to follow along with their partner.

"First person do double lan sao, left arm on top. Have your partner push on you," he said as he pushed down on my arms towards the ground. Mine didn't move.

"Now watch." He angled my forearms so that they were parallel to the ground. "Have your partner resist when their arms are flat." My shoulders gave out and I couldn't resist his downward pressure. He pushed my arms down immediately.

"Now, angle your arms up slightly," he coached. I angled mine so that my forearm was at an approximate 25 degree angle. "Now push on your partner," he instructed, pushing down on mine as he spoke.

He couldn't push mine down at all. I didn't feel any pressure in my shoulders. Instead, it felt like he was pushing into my feet. He asked me to go around and help ensure others were doing it correctly.

After a few minutes he asked us to try something else.

"Start with left on top," he began. He asked everyone's partner to push on the double lan sao like before. People could resist, no problem.

"Now do double sut sao," he said as he executed a throat killing hand, "and come back right on top. Have your partner push again."

People did and everyone could resist the pressure.

"How is it?" he asked.

"Strong," we said.

"Now, same person. Left hand on top, partner push, sut sao, come back with left hand on top, partner push."

This time everyone pushed their partner's arms down easily. People shook their heads in wonder.

Sifu laughed. "Not working? Try again, left on top then right on top. Then try again left on top and come back with left on top"

Everyone did, with the same results.

"Why?"

No one knew.

"What side of your body does the left side of your brain control?" Sifu asked.

"Right."

"What side of your body does the right side of your brain control?"

"Left."

"Exactly. The left side of your brain controls the right side of your body. The right side of your brain controls the left side of your body. You can't only use one side. You will be off balance. Makes sense to you?"

It did. But the demonstration of it was impressive, as was his understanding of body mechanics.

"You have to train both sides. On the street you can't say, 'Wait, try again. Attack me on my right side. I'm really good on that side."

It reminded me of the martial arts instructor Rex, who teaches Rex Kwon Do in the movie *Napoleon Dynamite*. Rex, wearing stars and stripes balloon pants and Karate top, is demonstrating a move. *Grab my hand*, he tells Napoleon.

Napoleon grabs his hand.

Other hand, Rex says.

Napoleon switches hands.

MY other hand.

"Right side, left side. You have to do both. People always work on their dominant side, they don't like to work on the opposite side. But what happens if you get injured? You broke your arm. Maybe you get cut with a knife. What happens? A lot of people don't understanding. You gotta work the other side."

Sifu went on to explain more concepts about the center line — an imaginary line running head to toe in the center of your body.

"Don't cross your center line. You would never reach across yourself with your right hand to get something out of your left pocket," he kidded. "Don't cross over, don't over-extend."

He walked over to a pair of Wing Chun Butterfly Swords and demonstrated movements from the *Baat Cham Do* form. He moved swiftly and gracefully, his hands close together, the blades a blur, extending and darting, cutting and slicing in rapid, smooth strokes.

He set the swords down and demonstrated the same movements with his empty hands. Once complete, he said, "Learn to use both hands, close together, like the wings of a butterfly. Can a butterfly fly with just one wing?" He shook his head and grinned. "Course not. Crashing," he said, miming it.

"It won't work with just one wing. No way. Your two hands are like antennae, they tell you where to go and pick up signals. They are for sensitivity. If you tense them up, you lose that sensitivity, the signal. They are also friends. The one will tell the other where to go, like a lookout."

Someone asked him what he meant by that.

"Stick to your station." He demonstrated a tan sao. "That's your station." He demonstrated a bong sao. "That's your station." He moved his elbow out so he was off the center line. "That's not your station. Elbow doesn't move. Everything stays on the center. Lead hand is there already, follow that lead hand. Why create a new path?"

That would be like the lead guy in a jungle wielding a machete to create a path, and the guy behind him deciding not to follow but instead cut his own path. The lead hand tells the other hand what to do, where to go.

"Wing Chun is very picky, very precise. But don't worry about right or wrong. It's really about the consequences of what you do. It's about cause and effect. Some things you have to find out for yourself. What is the consequence of this? What is the consequence of that? What difference does it make if you do this or that?"

Back to repetition, doing something over and over until it is embedded.

"You have to discover it for yourself, otherwise you'll never know, and it won't be part of you. You always need to investigate, ask questions, see what works on different kinds of people. If it works on everyone, then do it. If it only works once in a while, then you better find something more effective."

Sifu's easy confidence was a result of trying and seeing what worked on thousands of people over decades of study and practice, built on centuries of inquiry and testing.

He had us go back to drilling, offering a number of different exercises. In one he asked our partners to face us and push our left hip with their right arm.

"Now, where do you focus?" he asked those of us who were being pushed.

There were various answers.

"If your partner pushes on your left hip with his right arm, focus on his right hip. You will cross his center line, and close the triangle. If you focus on his left hip, you aren't closing the structure and aren't connecting the energy."

It took me a minute to work that out in my mind. When I could visualize it, I did as he had instructed. If I focused on my partner's left hip, I got pushed back instantly. If I focused on his right one, he couldn't budge me and I really didn't feel much pressure from him at all.

My partner did the same thing. We both shook our heads in wonder. Body mechanics was more than just what you did with your body, it was what you did with your body and your mind.

"What if you aren't in control of the center line?" someone asked.

"Even if you are not in control of the center line, control it mentally. In your mind you can always be focused on your center.

"Your mind is so powerful. But you have to use the whole thing, not just half," he said, panning the group. "You visualize it, you get used to it. Same thing in your form. Just don't go through the motion. Who cares if you do this?" he asked, blindly going through the movements while looking around. "Understand what you are doing, why you are doing, how you are doing. Put your energy through his center line, past his feet. Connect the triangle."

Sifu called two people up, Rob and Chris. He asked Chris to extend his left hand in a tan sao. He had Rob place his right hand on Chris' in a fook sao position. "Now, one thing so important, you need to understand the triangle." Sifu tapped Rob on the left shoulder then the right, then touched Chris on the center of his chest. "Chris, test his tan sao."

Chris drew his fook sao in and Rob was pulled forward.

Sifu then touched Rob's left shoulder, Chris in the center of his chest, then Rob's left shoulder. Once again he instructed Chris to test Rob's tan sao. This time Rob didn't budge and remained firmly rooted.

"What's the difference?" Sifu asked.

"The first one you crossed the line," someone answered.

Sifu smiled. "Exactly. The way you make the triangle is important. You have to understand and test, see what works. That way your mind makes the connections and can do the right way. If you don't, you can do something for 20, 30 years and it still won't work."

Me executing a pak sao with Sifu in Rochester 2004.

LESSON 29
LET ENERGY FLOW THROUGH YOU

The energy of the body and mind is very real and very powerful.
People get so caught up in it being magic or some secret technique.
It's not but you have to work at it.
We use all kinds of energy every day.
You may not understand it but you can use it.
It does no good to talk about energy if you can't use it.
Energy can only flow through when you are open.
When your mind and body are focused and relaxed.

"Look here please," Sifu said to the class as he walked over and placed his hand against the wall. "If someone pushes on you, your natural reaction is to push back." He asked the biggest student in the group to push on him as hard as he could. The student dug down and pushed. Pushing back, the veins on Sifu's neck popped, and his arms were taught as steel cable. After a brief struggle, he was pushed into the wall.

"If you tense and fight him, you will get pushed. Maybe you win, maybe you lose, but you will get pushed," he advised.

"Instead, think about this. Everything has a center. If you visualize that you are the center between him and the wall, what is he pushing against? You or the wall?" he asked.

"The wall," we replied.

Sifu lifted his left leg and sank his body down like a rock dropping to the bottom of a lake, extending only his right index finger to make contact with the wall. He bent his right support leg slightly and curved his spine, his upper abdominals folding over the lower ones. He extended his left arm and asked the student to once again push on him as hard as he could.

Try as he might, he couldn't budge Sifu.

"If you relax and let go, all his force will go into the wall, even if you are barely touching it."

How did his finger not break?

"Don't give him anything to fight against. This is not just physical. It is also mental and spiritual."

Guess that's why.

He invited all of us to try the same thing. We did, with varying degrees of success.

"If you are using muscular force, you are doing the technique incorrectly."

Most of us didn't know any other kind of force to use.

"This seems like a matter of faith," he said, "but not blind faith. Don't believe someone else. Try it for yourself. But make sure you are doing it correctly because in every movement there is the physical position, the mental process and the will or spirit."

"As you let your arms float upwards breathe in deeply," I said, guiding the 20 participants spread out across the hotel conference room, "and exhale fully as they gently float down like a feather."

In 2001, I brought Sifu into Kodak to partner with me in a program called *The Winning Mindset*. Designed to help employees understand and harness the power of their minds and bodies to reduce stress and increase collaboration, innovation and results, we held a series of sessions, each two days in length. One of these sessions was held in March for the US Sales leaders at Sanibel Island, Florida, not too far from Sifu in Atlanta, and very far from the Upstate New York winter for me.

At the end of the first day, we led the participants through a series of simple yet powerful Qigong exercises. (Qi, or chi, pronounced "chee" is a Chinese word for energy, and gong, or kung, is practice, cultivation or work).

"Now soften your gaze, not looking at anything in particular, and shift your weight to your left leg. Imagine that left leg is now filling with sand, like an hourglass, getting heavier and heavier, while your right leg is getting lighter and lighter as the sand empties."

After leading them through a series of movements, I asked them to close their eyes and feel their bodies, a concept foreign to many. "Simply stand and breathe with your eyes closed, imagine yourself sinking into the ground."

As I spoke, Sifu went around and worked on each person. He lingered over one woman whose face had that pinched look of someone who spent too much time worrying. He grabbed the air around her head like he was catching a mosquito and throwing it on the ground. He did that half a dozen times and then began making sweeping motions around her body, the movements growing increasingly larger. As he did, the tension in her face and neck drained away. She breathed in deeply and smiled, something I had rarely seen her do.

We wrapped up for the day. Instead of heading out, the participants gathered around Sifu like moths to a light.

"What did you feel?" I asked the woman as she headed over to Sifu.

She beamed and shook her head. "It was the weirdest feeling. It was like a weight just dropped off me." I could tell she wanted to go talk to Sifu, so I didn't keep her.

I moved around and chatted with some more of the participants. Their responses were all a version of the same reaction, that they had felt a sense of peace and lightness they had never before experienced. It radiated through their faces and bodies.

At dinner, everyone wanted to talk with Sifu, wanting to know what he did, and how they could get that feeling again.

"You have that energy already, inside yourself, and from outside. It just gets stuck. Thinking too much, analyzing too much. You begin to form patterns for what parts of your brain you use and where you hold tension in your bodies. I just helped you relax and flow. Nothing magic," he said.

It seemed like magic to them.

Someone asked him what the energy was like.

"Energy is like a hose. If you kink it up then grab on to it, the pressure of the water will push up against the sides. So to grab on it feels strong. But actually, that is not power, that is tension. The power only comes when you release the blocks and let the water flow freely," he said, making eye contact with everyone gathered, some seated, more standing.

"Containing is not power, holding on is not power. Flowing is power, flowing is energy, flowing is life. When you feel the hose as the water rushes out, that is power. It's almost electric."

That is what they wanted to feel again.

Two days later, Sifu and I had a few hours in the morning to kill before leaving for the airport to catch our flights. We headed out of our hotel and walked along the beach. The sun reflected off the deep blue water of the bay between Fort Meyers and Sanibel Island. Two seagulls were fighting over a piece a crab up ahead, and further out dorsal fins of three dolphins broke the surface.

We came to a bench and sat down facing the bay.

"Jim, thank you so much for bringing me down here," Sifu said. "You asked me if there was anything you could do for me and I said I'd like to do workshops for companies. I didn't think anything, but a week later you called me. I know you put your job on the line for me, and want you to know how much I appreciate it. I just sit in back and eat donuts, do a little bit."

I felt a lump growing in my throat. I owed him so much, nothing I could do would even come close to repaying him. Whatever I managed to get out in reply didn't begin to express what I felt.

We continued to talk about the two day session, how we felt it went and how we could improve. We had planned the vast majority of the workshop, but there were a few areas that were more ad hoc. I asked him what he was doing during the qigong exercises.

"I was getting their energy to flow. Their energy was stuck in their brain, they were thinking too much, analyzing."

"How did you know that? How can you tell?"

Sifu shrugged, pushing back his hair and clasping his hands behind his head. "I can just tell. I don't know, I feel it. In Wing Chun you will develop your sensitivity, so you begin to pick things up.

"When you tense up, all the energy goes up into your shoulders and chest. When you relax, your energy goes down. Like when you sigh, you breathe out, and relax everything, so work on relaxing, letting everything go down. A lot of people who sit at desks and look at computers tend to hold their energy in their necks and heads.

Then they get stuck, always thinking and analyzing and they overuse that part of their brain."

He could have been describing me.

"The energy of the body and mind is very real, and very powerful. People get so caught up in it being magic or some secret technique. That's crazy. It's not, but you have to work at it. You can't see TV waves, but you know they are there. You can't see the satellites waves that make your cell phone work but you use them all the time. So don't worry if you don't understand something as long as you can use it.

"Like a fan can move air, your mind can move energy. Energy is like water. Your body has water in it, but it is not yours, you didn't make it. It is constantly replenished. It flows through you. If water sits still, it's no good. Energy's the same thing. To use it, it must flow, but you must be physically focused and mentally relaxed."

"How do you do that?" I asked. There was a consistent theme to my questions, primarily revolving around letting go and relaxing.

"Do your first form slowly, like Tai Chi. The slower the better, take your time to really feel. First form is qigong. A lot of people talk about or write about qigong, but can they move four or five people?" he asked.

"In Siu Nim Tao, draw energy up from the ground, like your feet are suction pumps and you are standing in a lake. Then have that energy circulate up the front of you, up over your head, and then down your back to the ground again." He took a Kim Young Ma stance and demonstrated. "Breathe in as you imagine the energy coming up, breathe out as the energy circles and goes down." He stopped and beckoned me to try.

I kicked off my shoes and stepped into the hot sand. I visualized energy coming from the ground up the front of my body, timing my inhalation so my lungs were full as the energy reached the top of my head, which grew warm and tingly. I exhaled in concert with the energy traveling down my spine and into to my feet.

"Now, make it bigger. Go three feet below the ground, out three feet, above your head three feet, and behind you three feet. Like a ball of energy. Visualize."

I was a tree, rooted deep into the earth, solid, yet light and flexible in my upper body.

"Focus on my dan tian then?" I asked, moving my right hand to a space just below my navel.

He shook his head. "Don't concentrate on the dan tian. This can make your energy stick and make you crazy. Let your energy flow."

I practiced for a few more minutes. "Okay, good. Now, feel this." He was in a Kim Yung Ma stance and he guided my fingers into his stomach. "Push," he urged.

I pushed as hard as I could, but my fingers just got lost as his stomach muscles folded over on themselves. It felt like I could just go on pushing forever.

"Now, if I tense," he said, contracting his abdominal muscle.

I pushed him back immediately.

He smiled, "See?"

"Let your low diaphragm control your movements. Otherwise, you will use your hands and you will try to rush your movements, always anticipating. You will be anxious."

That explained why he always seemed so relaxed yet full of energy.

"If you let your low diaphragm control your movements, you won't rush, you won't be nervous. When you feel your energy rising up, slow down, or take a break. Let the energy sink back."

"Pay more attention to the energy?" I asked.

He nodded. "It can also save you hours of crunches," he grinned.

He motioned me over to the bench we had just been sitting on. "Jim, lie down on this bench, face down. Let me show you something."

I lay down on the bench. Through my shirt, he grabbed the skin around my upper back between his fingers and pulled, like I was a bloodhound. Except I wasn't a bloodhound and I didn't have extra, loose skin. I felt like howling like a bloodhound. Sweat poured off my face as I grimaced, wondering where this all was leading to and when it would end.

Then I had a rush of what I can only describe as electricity shoot down my back, as visceral a sensation as a school of minnows darting down my back. I got up with an unbelievable sense of lightness.

He brought his hands up into the chi sao position, one bong sao, one fook sao. We did rolling hands for a few minutes when I felt prickly sensation on my face and scalp.

"Your face is all red," Sifu said laughing. "Your energy is flowing better now."

I smiled and shook my head, wondering how he did this. I asked.

"Some of it you do with your body, some you do with your mind and some you do with your heart. Most people don't really want to learn this aspect. Of my students, maybe one out of a hundred."

I guess I was one, since I found it fascinating.

"Focus, concentration, relaxation, visualization, imagination, and letting go. You have to put them all together simultaneously."

A few months later I was working in my office. Joanne, a woman who worked for me, came in, her face as white as a sheet. In a barely audible voice, she told me that she had a migraine and that she needed to go home.

"Sure, no problem. Of course," I said.

But then I had an idea.

I asked her what she would do if she went home. She said she would lie down in a dark room, which in and of itself wouldn't really help, and that it generally took 12 to 24 hours for the migraine to subside.

I asked her to sit down and told her that I wanted to try something that might help her. I had attended a 10 week qigong class after seeing what Sifu could do, and I wanted to see if it could alleviate her pain at all. I had her sit down in the chair, relax as best she could, and close her eyes. I settled myself, breathing fully into my abdomen, and let myself sink into the ground. I brought my hands up and over my head then let my hands float down together in front of my face, my palms touching, settling my own energy.

Once set, I passed my hands over her spine then head, six to twelve inches away from her body. I sensed a low level of what felt like static electricity in most areas. When I got to the area in front of her forehead, there was a buzz about four inches in diameter. I gently grabbed the buzz and pulled, much like pulling cotton candy — gently, slowly. I let my hand drop and threw the energy away, as if throwing a crumpled up piece of paper on the ground. I did that about a dozen more times when all of a sudden it felt like a clogged drain freed up.

Her face pinked up immediately, and the buzzing sensation was gone. I finished with a couple of movements to seal her energy, and asked how she felt.

Her eyes widened, and she started laughing. "Amazing! I can't believe it. My migraine is totally gone. It was there one minute, and the next, completely gone." She stood up and asked me what I did.

I didn't really know other than feeling that her energy was stuck and pulling it out. That sounded pretty vague and new-agey to me, even though it was actually a form of qigong healing that had been around for thousands of years. It was only new to me. My response, therefore, was fairly general. The main thing, I told her, was that she felt better.

"Now get back to work."

"There are some things which can be sensed but not explained in words."

Chinese proverb

THE WANDER YEARS

I brought Sifu up to Rochester for a seminar in June of 2006, pretty much 15 years to the day after I first met him. It was well attended and his tutelage amazing, as always. He incorporated trapping to takedowns and ground work into the drills, which balanced out the stand-up work many of the participants were used to. I had a basic frame of reference from my wrestling days but it was still mind-blowing how he used the sensitivity and center line principles from Wing Chun to such effect on the ground.

At the end of the two days we handed out certificates signed by Sifu to all attendees. Each person came up to receive their certificate. Some bowed, some shook hands, some hugged Sifu.

When that was finished I made a few closing comments.

Firstly, I thanked everyone who attended. Without them I couldn't have brought Sifu up and so I appreciated their support.

Secondly, I thanked Sensei Matt Dorsey, who had once again opened up his school to host the event.

Finally, I thanked Sifu, or at least tried to. I made a few comments, but then my throat tightened up and I felt on the verge of tears.

What is happening?

"I love you too," he said, hugging me.

He had a flight to catch so we said our goodbyes and I drove him to the airport. He thanked me profusely, as he always did, which I thought was so backwards.

I thanked him again but the words never seemed enough.

I pulled up to the Delta Airlines departure doors, stopped the car and turned off the engine. I got his bag out of the car, and his brief-case. He always seemed embarrassed by me doing that but it was the least I could do.

We hugged and he said good-bye quickly as was his custom. "Okay, see you. Take care, bye-bye."

With that, he took off through the door with those same light quick steps I had come to know. I watched him walk away through the airport entrance with an unexplained sense of protectiveness like watching your kindergartener get on the bus for that first day of school. I knew he was street smart, tough and probably one of the best fighters around, but I also knew he was sensitive and caring and had a heart that felt more deeply than most.

That was the last time I saw him for nearly eight years.

I was still teaching but I had also started training in powerlifting. A big part of it was to have something to do with my youngest son, Danny, who was 16 at the time, and in the monosyllabic grunt com-munication stage most teenage boys go through (I certainly did). We competed together in powerlifting competitions and when it came to that topic we enjoyed deep conversations.

At the time I was Vice President of Human Resources for a $500 million dollar company and was involved in a pretty sizable acquisi-tion — over 1,000 people in 18 countries — and had six weeks to pull it off. As a result I was putting in long hours at home and abroad.

Then came another acquisition with a different company. This one much bigger. Five companies and 12,000 employees in 36 countries.

I made more money but of course with that money came more responsibility and time at the office.

And less time training.

Then I was asked to go on an ex-patriate assignment and relocate to Vancouver, Canada to help acculturate employees both there and in Israel. I taught as much as I could when I visited back home (Danny was a senior in high school so we didn't take him out. He and Jessie stayed in Rochester, and Rachel and Dave were in college). During my assignment in Canada, three of my students moved away — one to Florida, one to Texas, and another to the Air Force. Another stopped training and I was left with one student who drove an hour each way to train when I got home every five or six weeks.

When my ex-pat assignment ended, I started doing more functional training with a group of friends. We ended up going in 10 Tough Mudder races around the country — 10 – 12 mile races with military style obstacles designed by British Special Forces — complete with electric shocks, ice plunges, dives off high platforms, and crawling through mud.

I was in incredible shape, physically and mentally, and had a lot of fun.

Emotionally and spiritually, though, something was missing. Functional training wasn't the same as Wing Chun but I always figured I'd get back to it when things settled down.

The thing was they never truly settled down.

I got promoted again. More money, more travel, more people to manage.

Then another promotion, and...well, you get the picture.

Each year I would call Sifu on his birthday. The first time I reached him and we spoke briefly. He encouraged me to come see him. "We don't have to do Wing Chun," he said. "We can play tennis, whatever you want." He was reaching out to me, knowing that our relationship was the most important thing.

The trouble was that I hadn't realized that relationships were the most important thing. I still thought it was achievement.

I thanked him, said that it would be great, but never went down. I had been traveling too much.

Every November for years to come I called, but never reached him. Each time I left a message wishing him a happy birthday, and let him know how much I appreciated everything he had done for me.

Since I had stopped training in Wing Chun, though, the words seemed hollow.

That was pretty much how I felt all over.

*"A man travels the world in search of what he needs
and returns home to find it."*

George Moore

LOOK WHO'S HERE!

I reached what many would consider a high point in my career at age 51. I was Chief Human Resources Officer of a multi-billion dollar publicly traded company. I had a staff of 240 people in 36 countries, with a budget that was bigger than most companies' revenues.

Coupled with that position, though, was a relentless barrage of urgent issues. I lived on my blackberry. In the office at 7:00am, out at 7:00pm and doing conference calls with Asia most nights during the week. Travel was quick and often — fly in, take care of business — fly out.

By then our kids were grown, so they didn't need the attention like they had when younger. And Jessie was busy with her own career as a pediatric palliative care nurse and her jewelry business on the side.

We were both super busy.

She was happy.

I was pre-occupied.

I had accomplished a great deal. By then our house was paid for, we were debt free, and I had achieved my financial goal by that time in my life. Yet having that magic amount of money didn't give me what I wanted. This gnawing sense of discontent just beneath the surface didn't seem to abate no matter how much I achieved.

For some reason I never could seem to relax and seemed incapable of taking the time to enjoy all that I had. My "success" didn't come with that sense of inner peace I had so longed for as a younger man, the sense of inner peace I had felt, at times, when training in Wing Chun, and the sense of inner peace that always emanated from Sifu.

I slammed caffeine drinks like they were Kool-Aid, and more and more I'd have a glass of wine to relax at night. My hormone levels were shot. The ones that should be low, like cortisol, were high, and those that should be high were in the basement.

Even though, in many ways, things had changed a lot for me, I hadn't changed much myself. I felt pretty much the way I did when I first met Sifu in 1991.

When the student is ready.

Or maybe when the student is *really* ready.

I got a flyer in November of 2013. Kevin Seaman was bringing Sifu back to Syracuse for two days in January. He hadn't been back to upstate New York since I last brought him to Rochester.

I sent my fee in right away and started to practice anything that I could remember. The first form wasn't bad since I had probably done it thousands of times. Chum Kiu, the second form, was a little rougher, and Bil Jee, the third, was hopeless. I only remembered bits and pieces of it.

I remembered the Mook Jang (wooden dummy form) pretty well, a few of the movements of the Butterfly Knives form (Bart Cham Do), and of the 6 ½ Long Pole Form, but they were by no means smooth.

So I did my best.

I made the 90 minute drive to DeWitt, NY to Eric Winfree and Anthony Iglesias' school. It was in a wing of a mall which, instead of stores, housed a series of schools — gymnastics, fencing, CrossFit, Karate, a Kung Fu school, Tae Kwon Do, and Syracuse Martial Arts, Eric and Anthony's school.

I saw Eric right away. We smiled broadly at each other and hugged.

"Man, it is good to see you. It's been too long," Eric said.

"I know," I said, sheepishly.

We talked about the school for a bit when I heard a familiar voice bellow, "Look who's here!"

At 65, Sifu looked like he hadn't aged a bit, as fit and energetic as ever.

"Jim, how you doing?" he said, as he came over and gave me a hug, "How you doing," clipped and blending together as if one word.

I felt like I had come home.

There were over 70 people there. Kevin Seaman made his opening remarks much like he had 23 years ago back at Wells College. At 60,

Kevin too looked fit as ever, though he had shaved off his moustache and grey had replaced his once brown hair.

I partnered with Kevin during the seminar and things started coming back to me. With a newfound respect for the lessons and movements, though, I didn't try to rush through them.

At one point Sifu asked me to help other people, like I had years ago. Part of me felt like I was too rusty to help but then I realized that it was about them.

Maybe I had missed that the first time around.

The four hours went quickly and as usual, most of the participants went to eat afterwards. Kevin Seaman set it up so that I sat next to Sifu. I was slightly embarrassed by that. I felt like I didn't deserve it after having been gone so long. I was sure there were other people who should sit next to him, people who had kept up their training.

Kevin insisted, and Sifu came and sat down.

I found out he got married to Tracey, who accompanied him on the last seminar to Rochester, and that they had a baby girl. Sifu showed me the pictures of his daughter, Katie, and videos of her putting puzzles together. She was a little cutie, and smart as a whip. I regretted missing all of those years.

"Sifu," I began, not sure of what I was going to say, "I feel bad that I have been gone so long."

He shook his head, thankfully cutting me off. "Nothing to feel sorry about. What changing? Nothing changing. Like it always was."

I felt like a prodigal son of sorts and he was welcoming me back.

"I know you called me every year," Sifu said.

I wondered if he had gotten my messages.

"I didn't call you back because I knew it wasn't time."

I nodded. "I can't really explain why I stopped training. After all you have done for me…"

He again cut me off, thankfully. "Nothing to explain. You had to go your own way."

I felt like a weight was lifted off my shoulders. I felt like I had the chance, again, to learn from this wise and talented teacher and, perhaps realizing it for the first time, to have an amazing friend.

LESSON 30
REPETITION

Keep practicing over and over.
People ask me, 'How can I get better?'
Simple.
Practice. That's it.
Do it over and over.
Then it gets embedded in your muscle memory,
Your nervous system.
You will just respond.

"Keep practicing, over and over and over," Sifu said. "How many people here shoot?"

About thirty hands flew up. We were at an FFIA (Francis Fong Instructor Association) Camp, this one was being held at NuBreed in Queens, Alex and Luigi's school. Sifu had started the FFIA in late 2014. Each Association member gets access to a digital library of instructive videos ranging from one to seven minutes in length, covering a host of topics including belt level curriculums, drills and forms for each belt level. The videos also cover specialized training in chi sao, weapons and the wooden dummy, as well as recordings from live seminars. In addition, the membership includes three day instructor training three times a year in Atlanta. This fourth training in New York City was a bonus.

"Wow, amazing," he said, smiling. "People think shooting is easy. I tell you, it's not easy. Guys who are good ask you how many rounds you shoot a week. A week!" He scratched his head, "Uh, let me see. I think I shot about six months ago," he laughed and shook his head. "No. Not gonna work.

"Special forces guys, especially Navy Seals. They train and train and train. Focus on details. If someone doesn't focus on the details, people die. That's why they train so much.

"Then repetition. You have to do it over and over again. One instructor at the gun range shoots a million rounds a year."

A few people whistled in amazement.

"The guy has a sponsor but a million rounds. How can he not be good? People ask me, 'How can I get better?'" He shrugged his shoulders and smirked, "Practice. That's it. Do it over and over. Then it gets embedded in your muscle memory," he said.

"Your nervous system. You will just respond. You know the saying, getting on someone's nerves? The nervous system drives your body and mind. People always talk about controlling your mind. It's better to control your nerves. When your nerves change your mind changes. Then your body will change, too. Your muscles will begin to change. You will see for yourself over time."

He looked around the room, making eye contact with everyone.

"But be patient. Relax. Wing Chun is all patience training, discipline training. It's not gonna happen like that," he said, snapping his fingers.

There was that patience again.

"Some people say trapping doesn't work."

Trapping is, in simple terms, pinning an opponent's arm in order to strike, often times pinning both arms with one.

"What do you mean it doesn't work? That's like saying Muay Thai elbow doesn't work." He elbowed an imaginary opponent. "That working?" He grabbed his face in the part of the opponent. 'Yeah, it worked.'

"Like people shoot a gun. They miss, 'Oh, this gun not working. I better get a better gun.' They get a $500 gun, but still miss. Then they get a $2,000 gun. They have all these guns, but it's not working because *they* are not working. They are no good. Champion gets a gun from a pawn shop, $45 dollars, gets bull's eyes all the time.

"You have to do it correctly."

And you have to practice correctly to get there.

Pablo Casals is thought by many to be the greatest cellist who ever lived. Despite having attained unquestionable mastery of the cello, it is said that he practiced five to six hours a day up until his death at age 95. When he was 93, a friend asked him why, after all he had achieved, he still practiced so hard. "Because," Casals replied, "I think I'm making progress."

Sifu demonstrating a lock on Kevin Seaman in Cortland, NY.

LESSON 31
BE A SURVIVOR

We're not playing paddy cake.
This is about survival.
Shooting while standing there at a paper target
is different than a real situation.
Same thing in fighting.
Be a survivor.
No matter what, survivors get out.

"Wing Chun is street survival. Three seconds, take someone out. If you don't take someone out in three seconds you're no good," Sifu said. "It's different than a sport. In a sport, you have a winner and a loser. I don't really follow winners and losers, I follow survivors. No matter what, they get out. Fighter? You win or lose. Survivors always get through."

He had recently been approved to train SWAT members (Special Weapons and Tactics). "Training with these guys is different. We're not playing paddy cake. This is life and death situation."

A few of the guys in the room who were cops nodded their heads knowingly.

"These guys are big," he said, extending his hand as far overhead as he could reach. "Former Marines, guys used to combat. But up close is different than far away. You can shoot at a paper target. Being good at that doesn't mean nothing," he said, shaking his head. "You have to practice drawing from any position, from the ground, from a roll, after running up flights of stairs. Then," he said, pausing for effect, "then let me see you shoot."

He looked around the room. "It's different I tell you. One guy was 15 feet away. You know the statistics on cops getting knifed from close range. I tell the guy, 'I'm gonna attack you!' I rush him. He tries to draw and drops his gun. He goes to pick it up!"

A few people chuckled.

Sifu slaps the imaginary SWAT guy.

"Never, never reach down to pick up your weapon. I smacked him on the back of his head. 'Owwwhh' he says. Next time I'm gonna kick you in the face," he said seriously.

"I know the guy is pissed off at me. I tell him though, 'You are a professional. I could save your life.' Later on he thanked me.

"You need to train like the real situation."

Someone asked him how to balance realistic training with cooperating and taking your time.

"Good question," he responded. "You need to do both. Jiu Wan never let us hit each other hard. Just like this," he said, demonstrating a loosely held fist. "But we went out and fought all the time. Same thing in New York. Someone always brought a camera. Go fight and take pictures," he said, laughing.

"You need to help each other."

Sifu was quiet for a few minutes before speaking again.

"I am from Hong Kong. I don't really know China. I never been there. I appreciate it and where I am from but I am an American. If I have to put on the uniform and protect the country, it is an American uniform. Lots of problems here but I tell you this is the best country."

He spoke about the work he did with the Fort Benning Rangers. "People don't realize, but I never charged a cent. I wanted them to be prepared to do the job. It wasn't about anything else."

Sifu went on to talk about various aspects of street survival, including the legal implications of your actions. "You fight, always gonna be problems. No matter you are right or not. But make sure you survive."

Sifu Fong with SWAT team

LESSON 32
TRAIN HARD BUT NOT TOO HARD

You need to train hard but not too hard.
You have to understand timing,
gain sensitivity and use your imagination.
You are not going to do that if all you are doing is pounding away.

I had trained with Sifu each month since January through a combination of seminars, FFIA Camps, and private lessons. I had a goal of 100 hours of training for 2014 and with a newfound appreciation for the instruction, I was soaking it up.

"Wing Chun takes a lot of patience and time. It's not for everyone. People want to walk away dripping with sweat every time. They want a good workout. If that's all you want, that's easy to do. It doesn't mean you improve your skill."

That was me. I liked the feeling a hard physical training session gave me and had done that since I was 12 years old.

"A lot of people wonder why they aren't better in Wing Chun. I don't know," he said, though I bet that he had a pretty good idea. "Maybe they try to do too many arts. It's good, people should cross train, but you aren't going to master multiple arts."

Especially one like Wing Chun.

"Or they focus too much on physical training — working out, lifting weights, running — instead of Wing Chun training."

Oops.

"You need to train hard but not too hard. You have to understand timing, gain sensitivity, use your imagination. You are not going to do that if all you are doing is pounding away. Sensitivity, visualization, timing and relaxing are just as important," Sifu said, running his fingers through his hair, still jet-black and full at 67.

He must be doing something right.

"Wing Chun doesn't have rings, sparring. It's fighting. Sparring is fighting. It was developed over thousands of years. In the temple, nothing to do, just kung fu, trying what works, what doesn't work. They don't worry about money, house, nothing. Only Kung Fu.

"I wish I could do that," he laughed.

"Spirit first. Technique second."

Gichin Funakoshi

Simo Tracey Fong demonstrating Bil Da with Sifu

LESSON 33
QUESTION EVERYTHING

Hurry always makes mistakes. Slow down. Take your time.
Don't just learn a technique.
Learn body mechanics, then apply that to whatever you do.
Always ask yourself, 'What is the purpose?
Why am I doing this? When do I do this? Where do I do this?
The four W's first, then how.
Otherwise you will know the technique — the how —
but you don't know what you do,
where you do, when you do, why you do.

I took a few hours of private lessons down in Atlanta. Sifu and I were relaxing in his office during a break and talking about training.

"The most important thing is not how long you train, though," Sifu said. "A period of time means nothing, to be honest. You can do something for ten, twenty, thirty years and still not understand. If you don't have any connection," he shook his head, "it doesn't matter. You need to explore, investigate and test. Always seek to understand what you do, why you do, when you do, how you do, where you do."

His point hit home. I nodded my head.

"I know it can be frustrating. You need so many repetitions—thousands and thousands, over and over. But don't try to rush through the moves. It's better to take the time and understand what you are training for. Some people get so stuck in rituals that they forget what they are doing it for. They just go through the motions but have no connection," he said, shaking his hand and frowning.

It is easy to settle into a routine and stop asking questions, stop striving to get better. I admired Sifu's constant sense of curiosity, seeking out new ideas and ways to improve and deepen his connection and understanding of his art. He truly embodies the concept of the beginner's mind.

"Wing Chun can help you to develop sensitivity and awareness. First, you develop that sensitivity and awareness for yourself. You understand yourself. If you don't understand yourself, you won't understand anyone else.

"More and more, over time, with the right practice, your awareness and sensitivity extends to other people as well. When working with a partner, develop your sticking energy," he said as he stood up and extended his arms, beckoning me to practice chi sao or sticking hands.

"This sticking energy is the same energy you use to catch a fish," he began as we rolled our hands, alternating between fook sao, tan sao and bong sao positions. "Too much force and the fish will get off the line," he said as he pulsed his force forward through his arms.

I staggered back from the pressure then stepped forward and reconnected.

"Too little and the line will go slack," he said as he offered no force whatsoever, allowing me to move forward uncontested.

"Sticking energy you have to be changing, you have to adapt to the situation, but the energy is always there." His energy was dynamic, alive and incredibly powerful. It felt as if I was being alternately drawn in and repelled by a combination of magnets and rubber bands.

"To get the level of sensitivity needed in chi sao takes years and years of practice. In the beginning, most people aren't that sensitive. But, with practice, over time, it improves. In fact, sensitivity is the only thing that can improve with age. Strength will decrease, speed will decrease, but sensitivity increases with time."

But only if you work at it, I thought.

"In the beginning, you think all the time about what you are doing, so it is hard to be sensitive to the feeling. But over time, as you begin to relax, your sensitivity will improve. It will become natural."

We practiced chi sao in his office for another thirty minutes or so, then took another break.

"Chi-sao is a good exercise because it teaches you not to judge. If you judge in chi-sao, focus on an instant in time instead of looking at the entire person, you will get killed.

"In chi-sao you develop your intuition through sensitivity. You don't think what's right to do, you feel it. In your chi-sao practice, in time, you will be able to sense your partner's intent. You won't even have to wait for a physical movement. You just know. You accomplish without moving, know without seeing," he said. "The body should not be the primary focus. The body is secondary. Most never get beyond the focus on the body so never understand the art at a deeper level."

Sifu had been guiding me to that deeper level since the first lesson back in 1991. He had always shared those answers, he was constantly planting those seeds, even if, in my case anyway, they lay dormant for years.

We continued on to a more aggressive form of chi sao called poon sao. Poon sao, Sifu explained, meant testing, questioning, to see what you're made of.

The first time Sifu did poon sao with me we were in a hotel after a seminar. I outweighed him by a couple of pounds, had over 300 high school and college wrestling matches under my belt and had always excelled on my feet. In my senior year of high school I had a sectional record of 93 takedowns. Plus I was strong in the traditional sense having won a US National Powerlifting competition.

Given all that, you'd think I'd have done better.

But you'd be wrong, since Wing Chun isn't wrestling or powerlifting.

At one point I had to put my foot up to prevent getting driven into the wall yet again. As soon as I did, Sifu was moving backwards, ripping me forward, nearly yanking me off my feet. That first time Sifu threw me around like a rag doll.

This time I did only slightly little better.

"In chi sao and poon sao don't be anxious. Everyone wants to hit all the time, but don't worry about it. If you over-react with one hand then your other one will be weak," Sifu said.

He stopped, thought for a moment, and asked me to join him back in the training area. He walked over to one of the five wooden dummies — *mook jang* — and demonstrated four movements using only his right hand — *jop sao, huen sao, bong sao, tan sao*. The first two movements on the right top dummy arm and the other two on the left top arm. Then he switched to his left arm and did the same four movements, starting from the left arm to the right. "Look at my hip movements and my feet, Jim," he instructed.

His arm movements were perfectly timed with shifts in his hips and feet — *Ju Sun Ma* — sideways step, *Toh Ma* — advancing step, *Seep Ma* — intercepting step and *Toy Ma* — deflecting step.

He told me to try it, using only one hand at a time. As I began with my right hand, my left reached out instinctively, accustomed to hitting.

He nodded. "See Jim, that's why I am having you use only one hand. If you think about hitting, you will hurry through your positioning, your structure. Don't hurry. Hurry always makes mistakes."

Hurry always makes mistakes, I repeated silently.

I resumed the movements.

He corrected along the way.

"Slow down. Take your time. Don't just learn a technique. Learn body mechanics, then apply that to whatever you do. Always ask yourself, '*What* is the purpose? *Why* am I doing this? *When* do I do this? *Where* do I do this? The *four W's* first, then *how*. Otherwise you will know the technique — the how — but you don't know what you do, where you do, when you do, why you do."

"Yes, Sir," I said, and continued the dummy work for another ten minutes. All along the way he encouraged me to stick to the dummy and pin the arm into the appropriate corner.

"It trains you to press your partner's shoulder back in the socket, impacting their overall structure," he explained.

He demonstrated the same movement on me.

"If I drop my energy," he said, letting his voice trail off.

I could snap his arm down and punch immediately. There was no forward energy.

"If I stick to you," he said as he gave me the same energy as he had on the dummy. I felt his force all the way through my body. It pushed me back and down at the same time. Two directions were much harder to deal with than one.

"You control my whole body," I said.

"I control your whole body," he agreed.

He went back to the dummy and demonstrated a few movements, quick, sharp and decisive. He spoke as he continued to demonstrate.

"I can tell how good someone is just by listening. I don't have to see. It shouldn't be this," he said, hitting a dummy arm producing a low *thonk*. "It should be light, quick," he said, his movements producing a distinct sound.

"A click," I said.

"Exactly."

Sifu had me go through various dummy movements, focusing on sticking, and focusing on the body *through* the arm, not the arm itself. He coached me on the dummy for another hour.

Then Sifu brought us back to the middle of the room to resume sticking hands. After the sticking training on the dummy I was much more patient with chi sao, not rushed.

"See Jim, how is it?"

He asked, he didn't tell.

"Better, Sifu."

"Sometimes you need to go to something different to understand. If your student isn't getting a concept, try another way."

We continued on, switching in between chi sao and poon sao. "Never over-commit. Test your partner, sense the situation. See how he reacts, then go with him."

I tried a running hand — *jao sao* — and he corrected me. "Don't try to run, jao sao. Stick to one movement in one area and get that. Then advance to the next once you have the first. Get your basic moves down to start. Better to have five techniques that you can do from anywhere than one hundred you can't. Also, a straight hit is faster than a jao anyway."

We continued on with chi sao. He began a jop sao / bil jee movement (gate-closing hand and thrusting fingers) from chi sao and I switched my arm to counteract his movements. "Ah, don't change. You want to change hands. Why you want to change? You're already on the center. Stay there."

"Brazilian Jiu Jitsu says "Listen to their heart."
Same thing in Wing Chun.
Listen to their breathing. Technique can fake you out."

Sifu Francis Fong

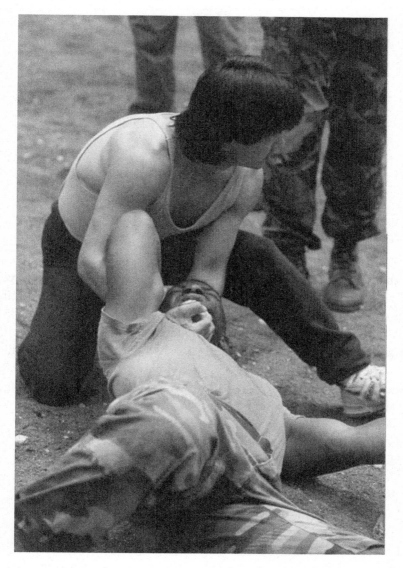

Sifu Fong demonstrating on a U.S. Army Ranger

LESSON 34
CONNECT, DON'T CONTROL

There is no enemy outside of yourself,
you are the enemy.
He is you, you are him.
Connect, don't control.
If you don't understand yourself,
You'll never understand anyone else.
See the real you, then you'll see others as they truly are.

I punched with my right. Barely moving, Sifu used his left to intercept with a sawing-motion cut punch. For the drill, I was supposed to circle my hand around his, a huen sao, but I was having trouble moving it. Although his cut punch was only from a couple of inches away, it felt as though my forearm had been smashed with an iron bar. I half wondered if it was broken. There is a saying in Wing Chun, "Muscles like cotton, bones like iron." I had just felt that.

I managed to circle, and he punched with his right hand. I performed a cut punch to intercept him.

"Ah, Jim. Sink."

He punched again and I cut.

He shook his head. "Don't chop. Chopping is against the arm. Cut the line," he said, meaning the center line.

I tried again.

"Better," he said.

I punched him and got the same iron bar to my forearm.

"I do hard to you. If you don't do hard to me, I'll do harder," he said, smiling.

He can do it harder? I thought. *Crap. I better sink.*

I sunk down and focused on the line, not his hand. I felt my cut punch penetrate through his body.

He smiled, "Good Jim!" he bellowed. "You got it. Now I switch the drill," he said grinning.

We changed to a *pak sao* or slapping hand back and forth. From there we progressed to *pak sao*, opening hand with *tan sao*, inside *pak sao* to the inside forearm, and strike with a *jing jern* or vertical palm. His pak sao caused red angry welts to rise up on the inside of my forearms.

"In the beginning, your pak sao is stinging, hard. It's good for the student," Sifu said.

It is? It doesn't feel good.

"It gets him used to it and gets them to relax. When you get tense you close up, judge, stop your thinking. That's when you get taken. Pushed, pulled, trapped, slapped. Instead of getting angry or frustrated, you should thank them. They are showing you where you are stuck."

I nodded. *Feedback.*

"But later on, you don't need to pak hard."

Would that be coming any time soon?

"Cupping on pak sao is difficult to move," he said, his hand gently placed on the inside of my forearm. I tried to slap it away, to no avail. He stuck like an octopus.

"Tension in a pak sao is easy to slap away," he said as he tensed his forearm, which I easily moved.

"In reality, you don't even hit. You flow."

He did the trapping drill again, this time more flowing and less pak-ing.

"Let each breath out be the end of that moment. Let go of the past, what you did, how you did, when you did. Start fresh with each breath. Don't give them any resistance, nothing to fight against. Sink down and relax. When your mind has no resistance, your body follows. You will notice over time, your muscles will be changing."

He stopped and squeezed my forearms and biceps, both of which were malleable. Nothing like the tense blocks I had when I was powerlifting.

"Good," Sifu said. "Getting better."

Little by little my body was changing. My muscles were becoming a bit like cotton (maybe a cotton blend). I had more work to do to get my bones like iron, though, even more work to do on my mind and the most with my spirit.

"He is you, you are him. There is no enemy outside of yourself. The enemy is you. When you touch, you are one. His move is your move, his technique your technique, his timing your timing. It's hard to explain. You need to go through the stages yourself."

"So then you can control him?" I asked.

Sifu shook his head. "Connect. Don't try to control." He extended his right hand. I did the same and he began *a lop / lop* — pulling hand — drill. He gently placed the heel of his hand on my wrist, his fingers the same, lightly resting on the inside of my forearm and wrist.

"Just connect. Don't grab hard. Wing Chun doesn't grab."

He then switched from using all four fingers to just his pinkie.

"If you use just your little finger, they won't resist," he said.

Then he squeezed hard with all four fingers. "Not like you go on a first date and crush the girl's hand to show how strong you are — 'I'm the man, baby!' See if she goes out with you again," he said, laughing. "I don't think so."

He reverted back to the light touch.

"Just connect. Sense him. Don't try to control. If you try to control, you already lost because you are thinking, analyzing."

This wasn't the first time I had heard this. *Did everyone have this much trouble?* I wondered.

"Be like water. Bruce Lee said, 'Be like water, my friend'. It surrounds, and can go through anything, even rock. Don't be like a rock."

"Yes, sir," I said, though to be honest I knew that these simple concepts were not easy to put into practice. Or maybe I just wasn't ready to let go enough to apply them, to let go of being strong, which manifested as hard.

Ultimately it was letting go of my ego.

"Water always goes below," he added. "It accepts everything."

I didn't accept everything, I knew. I absolutely tried to control.

"If you are like water, you go based on what?" he asked.

"Based on what the terrain is."

"Exactly, based on the terrain. If there is a rock, the water goes around. If you connect, you will know where he is going. Jim, look here," he said, adjusting my head slightly to the right. He pushed me — no, that isn't correct. I didn't really feel pushed. Rather, I felt an energy moving me in that direction.

"I moved you?" he asked.

I shook my head. "Not really, Sifu. It seems like I moved myself."

"Exactly, you moved yourself. If I connect, then I know where you will move, what you will do. Now look it here, la."

I don't know what the word *la* means in Cantonese but he usually said it right before he did something fast. Really fast.

He got in a right foot lead stance and extended his right arm in a *jong sao* — ready position. I thought he was going to do *pak sut*, which is a slapping hand with a knife hand strike. I was readying myself for a crashing force.

Instead, he barely touched my elbow, but I was, nevertheless, propelled back.

He smiled. I was tempted to ask him how he knew what to do but I knew the answer.

"Connect. Don't think of the other person as the enemy. There is no enemy outside of you. The enemy is you."

He waited a moment.

"The enemy is you," he reiterated.

"Use your practice to help you become a better person, that's the most important thing. If you don't, what's the use?" he asked, echoing his guidance from decades earlier.

He paused for a moment to let that sink in, as if to ask, *Are you ready to actually apply it now?*

"If I can train your body, I can open your mind, and if I can open your mind, I can open your heart. Everybody wants to kick and punch, they want to hit something right away. But until you work on your heart and soul, it is nothing. It's only on the surface."

"The attacker is not out there, but within."

O Sensei Morihei Ueshiba

Sifu on the wooden dummy (*mook jong*)

LESSON 35
YIN AND YANG

It can never be push-push, or pull-pull,
forward-forward, or back-back.
It is push and pull, forward and back.
Some days are good, some days bad,
Don't worry about it, that's the way it is.
You're going to have ups, you're going to have downs.
There is never only up, there is never only in.
You came from nothing; you go back to nothing.
You start from God; you go back to God.
Everything will come back into balance.
Yin and Yang.
Why worry? You won't change the way things are.

In a private lesson, Sifu Fong was explaining simultaneously parrying and hitting called *lin siel die dar.* "It can never be push-push or pull-pull, forward-forward, or back-back. It is push and pull, forward and back. Give and take. Take and give. Make sense?"

I agreed that it did, in principle anyway. "Yin and yang," I commented.

"Exactly. Yin and yang. One is going up, one is going down. Visualize it that way. That is life. You can't just give without taking and you can't just take without giving. It is a balance, give and take, take and give."

He continued to teach, incorporating the concept into various drills. "On gan da, it is not two hits. It is pulling and downward on the gan sao hand and forward and up on the hitting hand.

"Same thing with punching and your wu sao. Wing Chun uses the principle of yin and yang. Everything is yin and yang, heavy and light.

For example, when you hit, da," he demonstrated, "your other hand is in the wu sao position. The energy of your wu sao is up or light. If you project your punch forward, then that is not yin and yang because you will have an up and an out instead of an up and down, or heavy and light. That's your own style yin and yang!" he kidded. "The energy of your punch should be down and heavy, concentrating on your elbow, not your fist."

I practiced that a bit while he tested and guided me.

"Okay, watch your elbows," he said. "Your elbows have to be same distance from the body. Otherwise you will have one long, one short and be off balance," he said as he drove me back.

"Complete the triangle, first physically, then mentally," he urged, adding another geometric model to the mix. "If you are using tan sao, then your other hand is in jong sao. Tan sao can be giving energy forward, while your jong sao is receiving backwards. Or, if your tan sao is receiving, then your jong sao hand projects and can change into wan jern, or a hit — tan da. The technique isn't as important as completing the triangle and the flow of the energy."

How does he put all of this together so quickly? I wondered.

Later, over lunch, he continued his instruction. "Balance is physical, it is yin and yang. Heavy and light, light and heavy. There has to be a balance all the time.

"Life is a balance. You breathe in, and you breathe out. Too much breathing in, and you hyperventilate. Too little and you turn blue. If you eat too much, you gain weight. Too little, and you waste away. So how much movement is correct?"

"Just enough," I answered.

"Right. Just enough, not too much, not too little. How do you know?"

I shrugged. "Trial and error. You do too much, or not enough, and make corrections."

"Yes. Experience. Sometimes you hit, sometimes you wait. It's not just about hitting, it's about timing. What is better, hitting or waiting?"

"It depends, Sifu."

He smiled and nodded. "Exactly. It depends. Yin and yang is the way of nature. Man and woman, night and day, light and dark. Each needs the other, each exists because of the other. If there is no day, then there is no night. If there is no light, there is no dark. If there is no male, there is no female. Makes sense to you?"

I agreed that it did.

"You think you will go to work and have only good days? If so, your boss doesn't need you anymore. He'll do the job himself, no headaches. Some days are good, some days bad, but they're all good, make sense?"

Again I agreed, though not sure I was at that point in how I viewed things.

"Don't worry about it. You're gonna have ups, you're gonna have downs. Big deal. That's the way it is."

He told me about some financial issues he had dealt with a while back. He had gotten involved in some real estate investments with partners who had suddenly backed out. "People say they have money problems," he said grinning. "I ask how much. They tell me. Never even close to what I had."

"Oh, a lot?" I said, not really asking but curious nonetheless.

He told me a figure that made my jaw drop. I knew he had done well in the stock market and real estate, but this was more than I had ever imagined.

He shrugged. "Money comes, money goes. It's nature. You can't stay soft forever, you can't stay hard forever. Within soft is hard and within hard is soft. If you sleep on a concrete floor, you tell me how you feel when you wake up. The same thing with a really soft mattress, your back is a mess. A firm mattress is better, not hard, not soft, but firm. In the middle.

"If something can make you happy then another thing can make you unhappy. If there is happiness, then there must also be unhappiness. Yin and yang."

He was quiet for a moment before he spoke again. I could tell what he was saying was from experience.

"There is no taking without giving. If you want love, you have to give it. But what kind of love do you give? There are two kinds, conditional and unconditional. If you give conditional, what do you think you get?"

"Conditional," I answered, wondering which I more often gave.

"Just give unconditional love."

"In life we cannot avoid change, we cannot avoid loss. Freedom and happiness are found in the flexibility and ease with which we move through change."

Buddha

LESSON 36
BE HUMBLE

Never underestimate your opponent.
Don't play around.
Be humble.

"I was so cocky when I was younger," Sifu said, smiling and shaking his head. He was up in Rochester, NY for a weekend Wing Chun seminar. "When I was younger, my brother Danny and I got into an argument. I challenged him to a fight. I had been training martial arts so I figured there's no way he's gonna win. But he kicked me in the groin. I went down in one shot," he said laughing. "I remember curling up into a ball under my bed. It taught me a lesson, never underestimate your opponent."

I remembered the time I got kicked in the same place. It wasn't a sparring day so I didn't have a cup on. One of the other Tae Kwon Do black belts had been out of the dojang for about three months. He had been side-kicked in the jaw during a tournament and was injured pretty badly. That day he came back. He was our heavyweight and had a deceptive round house kick. It started like a front kick and then he flipped it over at the last moment. Well that day he didn't flip it and his big foot crashed right into my...well, you know.

Luckily I was right near the door. I went through the door and collapsed on the stairs. For two days I was in such incredible pain.

Yeah.

Sifu told us about another time when he was younger, practicing in Hong Kong. Six of the students held down another whose nickname was *Giant*. They asked Francis to pull off Giant's pants and hang them on the outside clothesline. Since he was the youngest he did. "As I looked outside, I noticed my Sifu coming back, so I warned everybody and we all started practicing Chi Sao." He said Giant came up from behind and struck him with a palm in the kidney. "I felt like I had been shot." Just then, he said, Jiu Wan came in. "When he saw my face he asked what had happened and the Sihings told him. He told me to go to the bathroom and drink cold water right away. Then I lost consciousness. Afterwards I was so weak I couldn't move," he said. "My Sifu yelled at Giant, but it was too late. Later on Giant apologized for reacting in anger."

Sifu Fong was unable to train for three months because of breathing problems. His Sifu sent him to a Chinese herbal doctor. He couldn't go to the hospital because they would have thought that his injury was from gang fighting and he didn't want his parents to find out. "So I was given herbal medicine. That made me realize not to play around.

"But really. I look at Guro Dan. He knows so much about martial arts, like an encyclopedia. He trains every day. His dedication and discipline are truly inspirational. Yet he is so humble, I tell you."

At the end of the weekend I called the group together, passed out the certificates, and thanked everyone for coming. "Without you, we couldn't continue to bring Sifu up, so thank you again," I said with deep gratitude.

Sifu nodded his head. "Really appreciate everyone for coming. Without you I am nothing."

"Be the energy you want to attract."

Unknown

LESSON 37
LET YOUR SPIRIT GUIDE YOU

You can let your body direct your mind,
And let your mind direct your spirit.
Or, you can let your spirit guide your mind,
And let your mind lead your body.
One way leads to hell, the other to heaven.
If you let yourself be ruled by your body, you are an animal.
If you let yourself be ruled by your mind, you'll go crazy.
Better to let your heart rule you. Your heart will never mislead you.
You can be an angel or an animal.
It's up to you.

During a seminar in Rochester, a few students from another Wing Chun school came. They asked Sifu Fong to look at their forms. There were portions that were quite different from how he teaches. He told the person they were doing well.

"I can't say something is right or wrong. Different teachers are doing different ways."

Later, as I was driving him back to his hotel, he elaborated. "Someone asks me what I think about another teacher's style, I'll always say, 'He's doing good.' Why should I say anything else? If someone pays me for consulting then I will tell them. But otherwise, I'll agree.

"People want to trap you, see what you think, so they can speak badly about someone else. What for? What's the use? They do what they do, I do what I do. Don't worry about somebody else. People get so caught up in drama, spending all this time on the internet. Me, I'd rather be training," he said, glancing out the window.

I agreed that some people wanted to stir up controversy. "You seem to let things flow off you pretty easily, though," I said. I knew that he had been through a lot in his life, yet always seemed unfazed.

"How do you do that?"

"You can let your body direct your mind and your mind direct your spirit," he began, looking directly at me. "Or, you can let your spirit guide your mind and your mind lead your body. One way leads to hell, the other to heaven."

He paused to let that sink in, looking out the window once again.

"You can be an angel or an animal. It's up to you. If you let yourself be ruled by your mind, you'll go crazy. Better to let your heart rule you," he said, placing his hand over his heart. "The heart will never mislead you.

"Everyone teaches the same thing. Buddhism is about emptiness. You're born, you die. You hold on and you suffer. Just try to do good things in this lifetime. Taoism is about letting go, letting things come naturally, in their own way, according to nature. Christianity is about serving others, putting them before you, humbling yourself."

Start with the spirit.

"Angel or animal. You have to decide."

*"It is only with the heart that one can see rightly;
what is essential is invisible to the eye."*

Antoine De-Saint Exupery

LESSON 38
LET GO

The sky, sun, air, water. Everyone gets the same thing.
Nature is a gift from God.
If people don't realize this they are missing the whole thing.
We have been given everything we need.
If you are always calculating, always looking to get, you will never open up.
Sometimes, the more people get the more they hold on.
They are afraid of losing what they have.
They get nice things and they worry — what if it gets stolen?
They aren't really happy.
It's okay to have nice things but the grasping is the problem.
You have nice things, great, enjoy them, but let them go.
Let go of what you are holding on to. Open your heart.
Sacrifice. Don't expect anything. Let go.

For years Sifu worked as a healer, applying various manipulative techniques to promote and direct the Qi throughout the body's Qi chan-
nels. As I had experienced first-hand, his work helped his clients' Qi
flow in a balanced and unobstructed manner, optimizing their holistic
health and maintaining a strong sense of well-being. Sifu's clientele
included a diverse background of people, ranging from sports person-
alities to executives and pilots for NetJets, Inc.

He also conducted a popular seminar — *Energy for Health, an
Oriental Perspective*, which demonstrated control of energy techniques
and use of energy to improve the total well-being of the client's mind,
body and spirit. Sifu's seminar was an integral part of the Labyrinz
Human Empowerment Training Workshops held at the LifeSpan
Health Center in Hilton Head Island, South Carolina.

Sifu and I were having lunch at a restaurant near his academy after
a private lesson. "He called me magic man," he said, laughing, talking

about the work he did with the CEO of NetJet. "I worked on him wherever he was. They come pick me up in a private jet. Fly me to London, Chicago, all over."

That quickly spread to doing work with other people at the LifeSpan Health Center.

"One guy, for 23 years his fingers had been curled up from a stroke. He said that the best doctors in the world told him that nothing could be done.

"I tell him, I'm not better than the doctors. I can't do what they do. I'm helping you to be open, to be open to God. Have faith in God, faith in yourself, and trust me. You don't have to have faith in me, I'm just a man, but trust me."

After one treatment his fingers straightened out.

"Another guy says, 'When I see you, I feel great.' He asks how much he should pay me. I say 'Pay whatever you feel you should. Don't calculate.'"

Sifu squeezed a lemon over his salmon.

"He said that he has so much money, he's a billionaire."

"Wow."

Sifu nodded. "The king of the mountain." Sifu took a bite of his fish. "He gives a lot of money to his family but they don't come around no more. He's been divorced three times. The third marriage lasted eight days. He lives by himself. He had a daughter who died in her early twenties."

"That's terrible," I said, unable to imagine the pain of having a child die before you.

Sifu nodded in agreement. "He said, 'If I have any problem in my business life I just write a check and it disappears. But my health, I can't do it. My relationships, I can't do it.'"

We both ate for a while in silence, pondering.

"Sometimes, the more people get, the more they hold on," Sifu said. "They are afraid of losing what they have. They get a nice car, and they worry — what if it gets hit? What if it gets stolen? They aren't really happy.

"It's okay to have nice things but grasping, trying to hold on, is the problem. You have nice things, great, enjoy them, but let them go.

Somebody asks me to borrow money, I give it to them and never expect it back. But, if someone asks that person for something, they should give it.

"Sometimes people tell me, 'Oh, Sifu. I'm really sorry. I can't pay you back,' and they are sincere. I say, 'Don't worry about it. It's okay. A lot of people have helped me in my life, so now I help you. Later on, if someone needs your help, you help them.' That way, from one act of kindness, that person can affect someone else, and then someone else. It spreads.

"Be positive. People want that energy."

Sifu's positive energy is one of the things that attracts so many people.

"Think of Tony Robbins. Why do people go see him? Because of his energy. That's why when I do healing I never criticize. Never," he emphasized. "Even if I know something is wrong. If I say something negative, they feel worse. Their energy is worse than when they came in."

Sifu went on to describe one patient at the clinic, a woman who was told by multiple doctors that she had less than six months to live. "She didn't want to be healed, she just wanted to be at peace. I worked with her and she is still alive today, over 10 years." He just smiled.

"It's amazing, I tell you. People say to me, 'Maybe you should teach healing. We can set you up with a clinic.' I could make a lot of money, but I say no. Nothing to teach, I tell them. I don't even know how I do it," he said with a shrug. "It's a gift from God. Ask him. For myself, healing came from Wing Chun. People ask me what style of healing I do. I say, 'I don't know. I have no style. I just do it.'"

He laughed. "Maybe I learned from healing myself. I tell you, when I was a kid I was crazy."

Sifu was the sixth child in a family of 11 — 5 older and 5 younger. "I was always out of the house. If I stay inside there's always fighting — fighting with older ones, fighting with younger ones.

"When I was seven years old I used to soap the driveway in Hong Kong. I slide down the driveway on my back. After a while it was too easy and I got bored, so I stood up."

I laughed, knowing what was coming next.

"I landed right on the back of my head. I had a huge egg," he said, holding his hand a couple of inches from his skull. "I was scared to tell my parents, so I got a needle, put it through a flame like I saw on TV, and poked it to drain the fluid.

"People always wonder how I know how to fix things — dislocated knees, jaw, shoulders — it's because I fixed my own. I used to play soccer and we didn't wear any shin guards. My shins all swollen, black and blue. My knee," he said, pointing below his patella, "was all the way down here. I fixed it myself. Jaws, shoulders, I can do no problem."

Sifu touched his right eyebrow. "I was living in Smyrna, not too far from here. I worked in a restaurant and these guys come in looking for my friend who worked there. These guys sold drugs. I threw them out.

"Later, they were waiting for me. Seven guys, they were hiding. It was dark, I can't see anything. I get into my car and this guy rushes up and punches me in the head with brass knuckles through the window. Skin is coming off. Blood everywhere.

"I go down in my seat. He thinks I'm knocked out but I'm getting my nun-chucks on the floor of the car. I get out — I want to kill him. I'm crazy at that time. I'm 25, I don't care. I have no family. In New York, people come in every day to challenge us. We fight all the time, throw people down the stairs. I'm used to it.

"Then cop cars everywhere. Lights flashing. The guys all run. The cops look at me all bloody, ask if I want to go to the hospital. I say no," he said, laughing.

"Later on I'm looking for that guy. I drive around all night. I go into a bowling alley where I know he hangs out. All drug related guys there. I'm wishing I called my friends up in New York, my army.

"I know he is there but nobody says anything. Someone calls the cops. They say that the Chinese gang is coming. The Tongs," he said laughing. "People always used to say, 'Don't go to Jason Lau or Francis Fong. They are Tong,'" he said laughing.

"Police come and the police chief takes me downtown. He is friends with the manager of the restaurant where I worked, and asks him about me. My manager vouches for me but still the Police Chief tells me to get out. 'I'm not saying you did anything wrong but you have 48 hours to get out of my town. I don't want any trouble here, and if you stay, there's gonna be trouble. If I catch you here again, I'll throw you in jail.'

"Y'all don't come back now, ya hear?" I said.

Sifu laughed. "Southern hospitality."

"So what happened to your eyebrow?" I asked.

"I put some Chinese powder on it — healing good — you can't even tell." There was no visible scar.

He was silent for a while. "I don't want to be a fighter, a lover, nothing. When you label, then you stop. Open your heart, let things come to you. If you have too many expectations, you limit yourself."

He waited a while before he spoke again. "Sacrifice. Don't expect anything. It will come."

"When you have a disease, do not try to cure it.
Find your center, and you will be healed."

Taoist proverb

LESSON 39
FIND YOUR OWN WAY

You want to be powerful?
The real power comes from love. God is love.
Some people go to church to feel God; some people go to a temple.
Some people sing to feel God, some people paint.
Some people practice martial arts to feel God.
You have to find your own way to God, to that love.
Otherwise, you'll always be lost, you'll always be searching.

Some days will be good, some days will be bad.
2014 had a lot of good days.

January 13th — our son Danny got a new job. A good day.

May 31st — our daughter Rachel got married to Josh. A good day.

June 25th — Rachel and Josh moved into their first home. A good day.

July 1st — Jessie and I celebrated our 30th wedding anniversary. A good day.

October 30th — our older son Dave and his girlfriend Nikki bought a house and six acres out in the country where they started *Lake to Lake Farm*. A good day.

May 20th — not a good day.

In October of 2013 I was made Chief Human Resources Officer for Kodak. This was on the heels of some very difficult years for the company, including successfully emerging from a grueling 20 month bankruptcy process called the most complex in recent history. Those years saw Kodak's workforce go from 20,000 to less than 8,000. It was a draining environment to be in day after day, especially considering the function I was in. Human Resources dealt with employees and unlike prior years, where the majority of employees were highly engaged and proud to be with the company, from 2010 on we were dealing with employees who were feeling intense emotions ranging from anger and fear — angry that their co-workers had been downsized and afraid it would happen to them — to despair and sadness — despairing that nothing they did was going to matter and sad that the company they once knew and loved was no longer.

The HR organization played a huge role in helping Kodak emerge from bankruptcy on time. That included spinning off almost 4,000 employees in 36 countries into a brand new company in a period of months. Kodak had a significant pension liability in the UK; the company negotiated a settlement with the pensioners and the UK governing body to sell the consumer portion of the company to the pension management fund in the middle of May of 2013. That meant we had to establish new legal entities in 36 countries (bank accounts, IT systems, payroll, benefits, leases, office space, cars...) by September 1 so the company could emerge from Chapter 11.

Teams all across the company pulled together and Kodak exited bankruptcy on time. I was promoted, basically in recognition of the job I had been doing for the previous 20 months, and was looking forward to helping revitalize this iconic brand.

With emergence from bankruptcy Kodak got a new Board of Directors. One of their first jobs was to hire a new CEO, which they did in March of 2014. He was very busy in his first two months and as a result I had only spent 20 minutes with him one on one, which was odd to me considering how closely I had worked with the other leaders of the company. It was common to spend hours a week together.

The new CEO said he was going to bring in some new people and make changes, which I thought was needed. The Chief Customer Officer, a friend of mine, asked me if I thought the new CEO would bring in a new head of Human Resources.

As it was a fairly typical thing for new CEOs to do I said, "It wouldn't surprise me."

I was wrong.

It did surprise me.

A week before Rachel was to get married, my phone rang. My assistant told me that Jeff was on the phone. I wasn't that used to working with the new CEO yet so I said, "Jeff who?"

"Jeff our CEO," she answered.

Oh, that Jeff. I picked up the phone and said hello in an upbeat mood. That mood quickly changed.

Jeff told me that he wanted to make a change in a senior leader position. In the split second before he told me who it was, my mind raced through a number of possibilities. Some of those changes, I thought, might be the right move, others I was worried about. I didn't think he knew anyone well enough to make that call.

Turns out he wanted to bring in a new Chief Human Resources Officer. Someone he had known for 10 years and worked with before. He apologized for notifying me via the phone but this new guy was going to start soon and they wanted to announce it. He wanted me to connect with him right away.

Stay with what comes.

He also told me that they wanted to announce the change the following Monday, which was the week of Rachel's wedding. It would, of course, be in the Democrat & Chronicle, Rochester's local paper. The last thing I wanted was for this to be a source of distraction during the wedding, so I negotiated a later announcement date of June 2, which was two days after the wedding. I didn't tell anyone besides my wife and my father until the Monday after the wedding.

He asked if I had any questions.

Did I have any questions? Uh…yeah. I could think of two or three. Since he had made his mind up, though, there really wasn't much to say. He told me that I could stay if I wanted, maybe do something in leadership development, but he would understand if I wanted to leave after being the top guy.

I said I'd think about it, but didn't need to. I had made up my mind the instant he told me. It was time to move on. Work had stopped being fun years ago and that environment wasn't something I wanted to be part of any longer. In addition, were I to stay, they would have to lay off two or three people to meet the budget and I wasn't about to do that to people who were, up to that point, my team.

Shit.

I got a name and phone number and hung up the phone.

My eyes went to my favorite picture in the world, one of Jessie and me and our kids when they were just 4, 2 and 9 months old that was hanging in my office. It suddenly felt wrong for it to be there. I took it down, along with the rest of my pictures, all of our children. Even though I would be around for a while yet, my overwhelming urge was to get the hell out of there. My feelings of loyalty for a company I had worked for and at times, especially lately, defended for 18 years, changed quite quickly.

Everything happens for a reason.

The Saturday wedding was perfect. Rachel looked gorgeous and happy and the weather couldn't have been any better — mid seventies, blue skies and no humidity. The rehearsal dinner, wedding ceremony, reception and brunch the following day went off without a hitch.

Monday I made all of my calls to my family and direct reports to inform them about what had happened. It was pretty straightforward and matter of fact.

Now what? I wondered.

Two weeks later, Guro Bill Hearst from Ottawa, Canada was bringing Sifu up for a weekend seminar. As it was only a four and a half hour trip, I drove up, passing through the Thousand Islands region shared by both countries. Bill invited me to dinner with his wife Tonia, one of his senior students Kara, and Sifu that Friday evening.

Bill is a very kind and centered guy. With long grey hair tied back in a ponytail, bright blue eyes, and that Canadian sense of humility, which was in stark contrast to many in the US, he reminded me more of a musician than a martial artist (he was both). The dinner conversation was pleasant, though I have to admit, my mind was elsewhere during parts of it.

After the dinner, Sifu and I headed towards the elevator. Turns out our rooms were next to each other. As we were walking, I told Sifu what had happened.

"Wow, I tell you, there's no loyalty," he said, looking at me with a mixture of concern and warmth. "How are you doing?"

The whole situation was still pretty raw. I had spent so much time focused on the wedding that it was just beginning to sink in.

"Good," I said, more reflexively than anything else. "Actually, I feel sorry for my team but it was time for a fresh start."

I had to let go. I had to use my art to help my life.

"You can get a job no problem."

I nodded, though I knew it could take up to two years. I told him that it had given me time to think, though.

"It's easy to fall into a trap of doing the same thing over and over without really understanding what you are doing it for. You have to figure out what you really want," Sifu said.

His comment brought me back to the very first time I met him.

Be your best. Master yourself. If you aren't happy with yourself, you'll never make anyone else happy.

We talked for a while more and then headed off to get some rest before the seminar.

The next day, Guro Bill picked us up and brought us to the Masonic Temple where the seminar was being held. Virtually all of Bill's students were there, as well as some people about an hour's drive from Ottawa. Sifu and I were the only people from the States.

During the next two days, Sifu demonstrated some of the energy work with others, moving them without touching, including making my middle finger wiggle back and forth faster than I could possibly do on my own. His abilities in that area were becoming much more pronounced. At the end of the second day students gathered around him to ask questions and tell him about certain aches and pains.

Bill's daughter was one of them. Celina was a stunning beauty. Almost six feet tall with the same bright blue eyes as her Dad, she had a powerfully muscled yet sleek frame. She taught yoga and looked every bit the part. Although she exuded an air of positive energy, I couldn't help but feel that there was a bit of sadness mixed in as well.

Celina stood up as Sifu worked, her posture perfect. She towered over Sifu as he moved his hands around her back and head. He then focused on her upper chest near her collar bones. Within seconds her cheery façade collapsed. Her face turned red and her eyes filled with tears. She wept for five minutes straight.

Most of the people had gone by the time he worked with her but she still seemed embarrassed by the flood of emotion. "It just hit me. I had been holding so much inside." She said she felt so much better, so relieved. You could see it on her face and body. Where before there was a wall, now there was an openness and calm. Her smile was genuine now.

Sifu had spent such a great deal of time working with people after the seminar that Bill was pressed to get him to the airport on time.

"Call me, Jim, let me know how things go," he said as he was getting into the car.

Driving back home I thought about what I was going to do next. My career path had progressed nicely up until that point. I had taken on bigger and broader responsibilities for years and had reached the top job of my field in a multi-billion dollar enterprise, heading an HR organization of hundreds of people in over 30 countries, with a budget close to forty million dollars.

Now I had zero direct reports in zero countries and a budget of nothing.

Stay with what comes.

I had a big title, big office and big pay.
Now I had no title, no office and no pay.

Follow through as it retreats.

For the first time in a long time, it seemed, I had the chance to figure out what I really wanted. Instead of just doing what I had always done I had the chance to figure out what I wanted to do, why I wanted to do it, with whom I wanted to do it, when I wanted to do it, and how I wanted to do it.

Thrust forward as the hand is freed.

I was given the opportunity to go back to my center, to find out what was in my heart and follow that calling.

To be honest, it wasn't what I did at first. Rather, I dove into the process of finding a job, much like I had done pretty much everything else in my life and the early days of my Wing Chun practice, with force and determination rather than sensitivity, patience and a focus on my center.

I had a number of interviews for Chief Human Resources Officer roles with multi-billion dollar multi-national firms. All were similar in scope and size to my last job with significantly more pay.

My ego loved it but my heart didn't. I felt I would be going down the same path.

In late fall, I was taking private lessons down in Atlanta and we again got to talking about my search. I explained where things stood.

He listened, as intently as ever, and told me I would find something.

"Everything happens for a reason," Sifu said.

I nodded. "You know, Sifu," I began, "For so long I have been working on being patient, on timing, being sensitive, letting things happen. As you know, that wasn't my strong suit. I was more about making things happen. Not exactly forcing them, but..." I said, pausing while trying to formulate the right words. Then I laughed, "Well, you know that."

He smiled. "Everybody works on that," he said graciously.

"I started out looking at this situation as a negative. You know, pretty pissed off about the whole thing. But if I think about it, it has allowed me to take time off, relax, and reassess my life."

Over time, though, I began to see the gift that this situation could be. It allowed me to train every day for three or four hours, to get enough rest, to be present with others, to be in less of a rush. It also allowed me to train with Sifu more than I had in years.

It allowed me to follow what was in my heart.

Maybe May 20th wasn't such a bad day after all.

That sense of peace and flowing began to seep into my daily existence. It wasn't dramatic, more like a gentle rain soaking into the soil. Taking its time. Like Sifu always encouraged.

So what did I want? I asked myself yet again. Somehow I knew the answer wasn't going to come through a logical analysis of my values and strengths, from thinking. I had done that many times over.

Somehow I knew it was going to come from feeling, from sensing, from letting go and connecting to a voice — omnipresent but never rising above a whisper, a voice which had been drowned out in my relentless pursuit of achievement.

My spirit.

"The most important thing is love," Sifu said. "The real power comes from love. God is love. Some people go to church to feel God. Some people go to a temple. Some people sing to feel God. Some people paint to feel God. Some people practice martial arts to feel God.

"You have to find out how to feel that love. I teach because I love it. You have to ask yourself what you really want. What will allow that love to flow through you? What is your center, what is in your heart?

"That is your path, to follow your heart. You have to go back there, to your center. Otherwise you just end up chasing. You end up lost. Just follow your heart."

I had come full circle, once again faced with many of the same issues that had confronted me when I first met Sifu back in 1991: to be present, to relax, to care but not be too attached, to be my best and help others be their best, to let love flow through me.

It had taken a long time, but I finally understood that the path of mastery is the one illuminated by your heart.

"Carefully observe what way your heart draws you,
and then choose that way with all of your heart."

Ancient Proverb

Sifu and I, November 2015

PART TWO — THE LESSONS REVISITED

The Zen monk Basho said, "Do not seek to follow in the footsteps of the wise. Instead, seek what they sought."

All of us begin by following in the footsteps of others — our parents, older brothers and sisters, and teachers. That is how we develop. To play music you start by learning individual notes and practicing scales and then progress to performing others songs. To compose your own music, though, you need to break away and go beyond — utilizing the notes, scales and structure to create your unique sound.

In Part One, you were introduced to a series of lessons designed to help you master your art and yourself, lessons that will be learned not upon reading, but rather when you make them part of yourself. I can't predict what it will take for you to embed these lessons into your life. As it is said, the best teachers tell you where to look, but don't tell you what to see. I can't tell you what to see.

In Part Two, however, I will show you additional places to look — further tips and strategies for achieving personal mastery. Keeping a journal will help you to track your actions and review progress.

LESSON 1: THE ONLY REAL FIGHT

Why bother spending years and years training in martial arts?
The answer is that even though you may never get into a fight,
you are always fighting yourself.
That's the only real fight.
Self-defense is good. Being healthy is good, too.
But if you aren't at peace with yourself, what does it really matter?
Use your training to help your life.

In your journal, jot down your answers to the following questions:

➤ What does fighting yourself mean to you? Getting angry?
Negative self-talk? Being disappointed? Engaging in undesired behavior? What are those situations where you find you aren't at peace with yourself?
➤ What is your pattern(s) of reaction?
➤ Do you tense up in certain parts of your body? If so, where?
➤ Do you talk to yourself? If so, what do you say?
➤ Do you get silent or violent (verbally, if not physically)? Or both?

The first step to changing any behavior is being aware of your current patterns.
➤ For a week, write down every time you feel you are "fighting yourself" — negative self-talk, being angry with yourself. Don't make a change just yet, simply notice and write down the situations in which you fight yourself.
➤ I fought myself when: _____
➤ My reaction was: _____

LESSON 2: BE YOUR BEST

Whenever you compare yourself to other people
You either think you are better, or not as good.
That way is a trap. It will never be enough to fill your emptiness.
The more you run after it, the more you will need.
It will never be enough because you will never be enough.
You will do better than others, others will do better than you.
Who cares? Just be your best. Be happy with who you are.

Guro Dan Inosanto has a wonderful way of putting things. At the 2014 Train with The Masters camp at the Francis Fong Martial Arts Academy in John's Creek, Georgia, he asked, "What if we were at a basketball practice and the first drill is reverse layup from the right with a dunk. Second drill is a reverse layup from the left with a dunk. Third drill is a layup from the right, switch hands and dunk, and the fourth drill is a layup from the left, switch hands and dunk. How many of you can do that? Probably none of us. We would have to adapt those drills based on our own physicality.

"Likewise, if you are 6'2", 240lbs, you're not going to be a jockey. There aren't a lot of horses that are going to carry you. If you want to be a jockey, you're going to be 5'2", maybe 120lbs with tremendous upper body strength.

"You have to adapt what works for you based on your physicality. What works for someone else may not work for you. You also have to adapt what you can do when you are 20 with what you can do when you are 40 or 50. I'm 77," he said with a full face grin. "The way I train now is different than what I did 20 years ago."

Part of "being your best" is to develop an understanding of your attributes — physical, mental, and emotional: how you think, how you take in information, how you learn, how you perceive the world, what you focus on and notice, how you engage with others, what drives you. Your attributes are based on your culture and upbringing (and associated beliefs) — *nurture* — and based on the way you are wired — *nature*.

Howard Gardner, author of *Frames of Mind: The Theory of Multiple Intelligences*, outlines 9 different types of intelligence:

1. Naturalistic intelligence — people who are sensitive to the natural world (animals, plants, weather).

2. Musical intelligence — people who are sensitive to sound, rhythm, timbre, tone, melodies, pitch.

3. Logical-mathematical intelligence — people with an ability to easily recognize patterns and numbers, use logic, to calculate and reason.

4. Existential intelligence — people who are drawn to questions of philosophy and existence, of why things are the way they are.

5. Interpersonal intelligence — people with an ability to get along with others, to understand others points of view, to be able to read body language.

6. Body-Kinesthetic intelligence — people who possess an excellent sense of timing, coordination and mind-body connection.

7. Linguistic intelligence — people who excel at thinking about words and phrases and express themselves verbally.

8. Intra-personal intelligence — people who have an ability to understand themselves, their emotions and what drives them.

9. Spatial intelligence — people with an ability to see things in three dimensions who can mentally produce and arrange images and who have excellent spatial reasoning.

People can score high on more than one area of intelligence.

What is **your best?**

> From the list above, which of the 9 intelligences do you possess?
> What physical attributes do you have?
> When do you feel at your best? In what types of situations? What are you doing?
> What have others said about your strengths? What have you been recognized for?
> What drives you? What motivates you the most?
> What are you naturally interested in?

For a week, commit to doing three things:

1. First, go out of your way to notice the gifts that other people have. What do you admire about this person? What can you learn from him or her?

2. Second, make it a point to compliment at least two people a day. Be specific — "You have such a wonderful way of greeting people — you have a beautiful smile and are so friendly, you make people feel welcome. Nice job!"

3. Third, at the end of every day, reflect on what you did well. Acknowledge yourself with the same level of specificity. It may feel odd to do but often people who are hard on themselves are equally hard on other people. You may find that as you focus on your best it will be much easier to see the best in others as well.

LESSON 3: NO ONE CAN GIVE YOU WHAT YOU DON'T HAVE

If you aren't happy with yourself,
you'll never make anyone else happy either.
No one can give you what you don't have for yourself.
You'll always be looking to get something from other people
to make you feel a certain way.

In 1993 I had the opportunity to meet John McCormack. An incredible visionary and captivating speaker, John is the author of *Self Made in America*, and was voted Inc. Magazine's *Entrepreneur of the year* in 1989. At that time he was CEO of Visible Changes, an extremely successful chain of hair salons in the southern United States.

John, however, wasn't always so successful. Born into a working class Irish Catholic family in New York City, as a "McCormack male" John had one of two options as a career as he tells it; he could either become a cop or a priest. Since celibacy didn't appeal to him he decided to become a police officer and joined the force at age 19. He was assigned foot patrol, walking the streets of Brooklyn.

One day, a couple of years later, he got a call that changed his life forever. He was on duty when he received word that there was an armed robbery in progress at a neighborhood grocery nearby. He raced to the store. With his weapon drawn, he entered the store, only to be met by three men armed with sawed off shotguns.

"Shoot him," barked one of the men, apparently the leader.

"Hey, hold on now," John said, trying to diffuse the situation and buy some time. "Look, you are surrounded. There are cops all over the place. You shoot me and there is no way you will get out alive," he said in what he hoped was a believable tone, since none of it was true.

They hesitated. Good sign. He continued, not wanting to lose his chance. "Besides, you probably didn't get very much anyway. I mean, come on, what did you get?"

"Twenty-eight bucks," one of the other men replied.

"Shut up," screamed the leader. Apparently a two-word combination was this guy's preferred method of communication.

"Twenty-eight bucks?" John asked. "You're willing to die for twenty-eight bucks?" he said, no doubt asking himself the very same question. "Come on, it's over. Put your guns down and I'll let them know you cooperated."

Through skillful negotiating and plain old luck, John made it out of there alive. But he was never the same. It gnawed at him that he almost died over twenty-eight dollars, so he decided to take a leave of absence from the NYPD and figure out what he really wanted to do with his life.

While he was considering his options, he and his brother got together to sell Christmas trees to make a little money. They rented a space in Manhattan, sold the trees, and they both netted about $3,000. John took his money and invested it in the stock market.

With what John described as a little talent and being in the right place at the right time, he soon parlayed that $3,000 into $100,000. He got into the business of trading stocks, and his personal portfolio grew to $1,000,000 by the time he was twenty-five. He was a millionaire, replete with two limousines, one for him and one for his friends.

Well, as the saying goes, what goes up must come down. Within a short period of time, John lost that million, plus an additional $250,000 that he borrowed figuring if he did it once, he could do it again. That didn't quite pan out, and he soon found himself a quarter of a million dollars in debt with no prospects of ever paying it back. He was not about to renege on his obligations but the best offer he got was a job paying $18,000 a year. Even if he saved all that he earned, with a wife to support, there was no way he was going to pay back what he owed.

Totally despondent, he decided to take his own life so that at least his wife could collect the insurance money to live on. He said that his plan was to swim out in the ocean until he couldn't swim any more. He was sitting on the beach screwing up his courage to do it when a voice called out to him.

"Your ship's not gonna come in there."

John looked up at an elderly man shuffling towards him.

Before John has a chance to respond, the man continued, walking closer. "Your ship's not gonna come in here," he repeated, "You gotta go to the harbor."

John took him for a babbling fool. "What are you talking about?" he asked.

The man stopped a couple feet away from John, reached down and extended his hand. "My name is Abe. Is there something you want to tell me?" he said in a clear, calming voice.

The question, the timing, and Abe's energy all hit John at once, and for some reason he answered. All his pent up frustrations and emotions came pouring out as he told his story about what happened on the police force, about selling Christmas trees, and how he made a million dollars then lost it. Then just after he told Abe that he was two hundred and fifty grand in the hole, Abe says, "You got fifty bucks?"

For crying out loud, John thought to himself, what a fool I am. This guy just wants a handout.

"You got fifty bucks or not?" Abe asked again.

"It's about all I have," John answered, "but…"

"Look," Abe continued, "I'll bet you five hundred dollars to your little fifty, 10 to 1 odds, that I can beat you in a foot race from here to that pier."

John was taken aback. The pier was about fifty yards away. John was twenty-six years old and he figured Abe to be in his mid-seventies. "There's no way you can beat me in a race," John said.

"What, are you chicken? Afraid of losing to an old man?" Abe prodded.

"No, of course not." For a moment John wondered if Abe was an Olympian from 1920 or something. "I just don't want to take your money."

"Fat chance. You willing to do it?"

By then John was annoyed. "Yeah, I'll do it," he said. "I'll take your money if that's how you want it."

"Great. But you have to put your feet in this," Abe said, producing a medium-sized canvas shopping bag he had with him. "Still think you can do it?"

"Yeah, I do." John put his feet in the bag.

"Great," Abe said, hesitating for a moment. "Oh, one more thing." Abe spun John around. "You have to do it backwards," he shouted as he took off towards the pier.

John fell backwards, cursed and got back up. By the time he got himself together again, Abe had already made it to the pier. John was angrily taking out his wallet as Abe sauntered back. Abe put his hand lightly over John's. "Look, I didn't come here to take your money. Keep it."

John started to protest then thought better of it.

"Think about what you have learned here today. I'll meet you here Monday morning at 8:00am sharp. If you learned what I wanted you to learn, I'll consider working with you. If not, I never want to see you again." With that, Abe left.

John walked back to his car scratching his head, his earlier mission forgotten, at least temporarily. Over the weekend he pondered the interaction.

Monday morning came and Abe got right to the point. "Well, what did you learn?"

"I gave it a lot of thought," John said. "I guess I learned that in any game, if you set up the rules, you can always win."

Abe smacked his own forehead. A broad grin spread across his face. "Fantastic!" he beamed. "I sent my sons to Ivy League schools and they didn't get that. They'll waste my millions when I die."

It turned out that Abe was a serial entrepreneur and self-made multi-millionaire. He was walking the beach that day because he had recently found out that his wife had cancer and had only a short time to live. He was distraught and didn't know what to do, until he saw someone who looked like he was in even worse shape than himself.

For the next two years Abe mentored John in the fundamentals of business. For all that he learned, though, John said no lesson was more important that the first one:

In any game, if you set up the rules, you can always win.

We all have rules that dictate how we feel, but few people recognize what these rules are or whether or not these rules support or prevent them from experiencing the emotions they consider most important. In general, there are three areas of which to be aware:

1. **The origin of your rules.** For many people, their rules are sub-conscious, the result of beliefs bestowed upon them from childhood (if I don't get straight A's then I'm no good).

2. **Overly rigid rules.** Often, people have rules which are virtually impossible to reach (to be happy, I've got to have 6% body fat, make a million dollars a year, and be perfect at everything).

3. **Rules where other people dictate your experience.** Just as often people create rules where others need to do things for them to experience an emotion (for me to feel loved my spouse has to always treat me a certain way, or for me to feel like I am a good mother my kids always have to be well behaved, or for me to feel good about myself my boss needs to tell me I'm doing a good job at least once a week…). What are the chances that other people are going to do precisely what you need at precisely the exact time you need it? Pretty slim.

Step One — Discover your rules.

To discover what your rules are, simply ask yourself either of the following questions:

What has to happen for me to feel _____ (like I am making progress, that I am learning, that I am making a difference…)?

Or

How do I know when I am _____ (making progress, learning, making a difference…)?

List out your rules for each of your values in your journal.

Step Two — Determine their origin.

To determine the origin of your rules, simply ask yourself, "Where did they come from? Did I consciously select this rule? Does it make sense to me? Does it support me in achieving my goals and living the kind of life I desire?

Step Three — Determine if your rules appropriately support and motivate you.

If your rule for making progress is, "Everything has to be simultaneously improving all the time," you probably aren't going to feel like you are making progress very often. If, on the other hand, your rule is, "I must become aware of how I can do better so I learn or I objectively improve," chances are you'll feel like you are improving all the time since you will either actually improve or you will make a new distinction in the pursuit of learning. If your rules rely on what other people need to do, you may be setting yourself up for disappointment. On the other hand, if you can control your rules, you have the power to determine how you feel on a consistent basis.

Step Four — Recreate any of your rules as needed so that they empower you.

As an example, an old rule might be: I feel great whenever I do something perfectly.

New, more effective rules might be:

➤ I feel great any time I learn and improve, even just a little bit.

➤ I feel great any time I make a mistake and as a result become better.

➤ I feel great any time I learn and then share that with other people.

In your journal, write down your Old Rules, and your New more empowering Rules.

LESSON 4: MASTER YOURSELF

Mastering an art is really about mastering yourself.
If you haven't mastered yourself,
it doesn't matter if you master something else.

What is self-mastery to you? What does it mean to master yourself? Allow me to offer a definition: to be aware of your own tendencies and capabilities — physically, emotionally, mentally, intuitionally, and spiritually — and to constantly strive to improve those tendencies and capabilities while accepting where you are at any given point in time.

So, what has to happen for you to feel great about where you are while striving to improve? Jack Canfield, Success Coach, co-creator of the *Chicken Soup for the Soul®* series which includes forty *New York Times* bestsellers, and author of *The Success Principles*, said:

It is very hard to produce a result that is bigger than the vision you have.

➤ What is your vision of Self-Mastery?

➤ What would you be like physically? How would you move?

➤ What would you be like mentally? How would you think?

➤ What would you be like emotionally? How would you respond to various situations?

➤ How aware would you be of your surroundings?

➤ What would your spirit be like? What about your sense of energy?

➤ How would you treat other people? How would you make them feel?

➤ If you were to master yourself, what specifically would be different from the way you are right now? Three years from now, what would have had to happen for you to feel happy about your progress?

Paint that picture of yourself as vividly as you can. In your journal, take some time to write down answers to the questions above that make the most sense to you.

"Can you walk on water?
You have done no better than a straw.
Can you fly in the air?
You have done no better than a bluebottle.
Conquer your heart;
Then you may become somebody."

Ansari of Herat

LESSON 5: RELAX, BE LIKE A KID

You have to relax.
Otherwise, you'll never learn.
That's why I'm always telling stories and jokes.
I want you to relax and enjoy yourself and breathe.
When you breathe fully and take your time, you relax.
By relaxing, you can learn better.
Be like a kid.

"What fires together, wires together". Originally coined by Sigmund Freud, neuroscientists found that our brains connect memories with feelings and emotions. The stronger or more unique the stimulus, the stronger the connection.

Think about it. Don't you have a song that, the instant you hear it, reminds you of someone? It transports you back in your mind to that person and time, and puts you in a great mood or a lousy mood, depending on the connection? You have those same reactions to places, people, even smells. Training movements with tension will hard wire the tension to the movement, which is difficult to undo. It's easier to start without tension and build gradually from there.

➤ When you train (or do anything), take your time. If you feel tension creeping up, take a break. Relax. Breathe. Smile. Laugh. Sing. Do something else. Come back to it.

➤ Notice where you habitually hold your tension. For many people it is in their neck or upper shoulders. Others hold it in the muscles of their face, chest, abdominal region or low back. Be aware of that tension (it is a habit!). Let it be a reminder to you to relax — breathe.

"The less effort, the faster and more powerful you will be."

Bruce Lee

*"If my heart can become pure and simple like that of a child,
I think there can be no greater happiness than this."*

Kitaro Nishida

LESSON 6: SINK

You want to be strong?
Be like water — relaxed.
When you relax, you sink down into the ground.
No one is smarter than heaven,
no one is stronger than the earth.
We are in between.
Relax into the earth.
Let him fight himself.
Don't fight against him

➤ Get in a relaxed stance. Imagine that you are looking down on yourself from above. Look at your surroundings — not just you but you in relation to everything else — the floor, the space you are in. Notice how much better you sink when you focus on everything including you and not just yourself.

➤ Practice your Siu Nim Tao form like that, watching from above.

➤ Throughout the day, use the same approach of looking down on yourself. Notice how it helps you to relax and sink.

➤ Wear ankle weights throughout the day. It will not only build up your strength, but it will also help you sink and relax.

LESSON 7: DON'T RESIST, REDIRECT

Where does water go, above or below?
Below, to the lowest level.
To redirect their energy, you have to go lower.
You have to put yourself below others.
When it comes to you, don't try to go over it.
Go below it, accept what he gives you and redirect it back.

For one week, write down your reaction when things don't go the way you thought:

> Do you tense up in a certain part of your body? If so, where?

> Do you say certain things? If so, what?

> Most likely you have a pattern of reaction when things don't go your way. Instead of going with the flow, you probably try to fight it. For a week, simply notice your pattern and record it in your journal.

"The stronger you become, the gentler you will be."

Unknown

LESSON 8: THE HARDER YOU TRY, THE WORSE YOU DO

In martial arts, if you try to kill your partner on every shot
you won't understand the basics.
It will be very difficult for you to acquire the sensitivity and
timing you need to get really good.
When you train, go easy at first.
Later, when you have the technique, you can speed up
and the power will be there.
In a lot of things the harder you try the better you do.
But in Wing Chun, this is not really true.
The harder you try, the worse you do.

➤ When you train, do you feel comfortable going slowly?
Remember, slow is smooth, smooth is fast.

➤ Have you ever asked your training partner to slow down? If not,
why not?

➤ What does it mean to you to go slow?

LESSON 9: LET YOURSELF MAKE MISTAKES

Let yourself make mistakes.
We learn more from our mistakes.
But you can't learn from a mistake until you make a mistake.
When you train, don't worry about winning.
In training make sure you learn as you go along, little by little.
1,000 out of 1,000 times you lose.
Then you lose 999 times out of 1,000, then 998.
Slowly, consistently, you learn.

➤ Keep a journal and track the number of mistakes you made on a daily basis. If you aren't making many (or any), you probably aren't taking very many risks, you aren't trying new things and you aren't growing.

➤ Determine what you learned (or could learn) from those mistakes.

➤ When you are training, try to succeed around 80% of the time. If you are working with a partner, make this agreement up front. If your partner is succeeding 10 times out of 10, it's not challenging enough. If they are succeeding only 2 times out of 10, you are making it too hard.

LESSON 10: LEARN FROM ANYONE

Train with different people in different situations.
It doesn't matter what skill level they are.
You can learn from anyone.
You will see your own mistakes in somebody else;
the ones you point out are really your own.
The more things you try with different people,
the more you will understand and be able to apply.

Early in my career I recall being invited to a meeting between my manager and an expert in the area of organizational change. It was a two hour meeting, and not once did my manager talk about all the great work she and her team had done. When the visitor left, I asked her why. "I already know what I know," she replied. "I want to know what he knows."

That commitment to learning and listening is the admirable hallmark of a great leader.

Here is an idea to hone your skills of listening and learning: At the end of every day, get in the habit of asking yourself:

➤ What did I learn today?

➤ Who did I learn from?

➤ How did I do asking questions to others in order to elicit their knowledge?

➤ How open was I to learning? How did I exemplify that?

➤ How did I express my appreciation for others sharing their knowledge?

➤How will I apply what I learned to help myself and others?

Make a point of once a week going and asking someone you would consider your junior for their input and perspective.

LESSON 11: CONSTANTLY EVOLVE

You have to evolve.
Even though you are a teacher,
you have to be a student.
People don't realize how much you have to keep learning.
I learn every day, try to get better every day.

It's easy to stay in our comfort zones. We're good there. But we don't grow there.

Helen Keller said, "Every day I do something that scares me." Make a point of routinely doing something that, if not scaring you, at least gets you out of your comfort zone:

> ➤ Take a class or course in something new.
> ➤ Learn a new language.
> ➤ Become a white belt again — take a different style of martial art.
> ➤ Go to a different restaurant, try different cuisine.
> ➤ Drive a different way to work.
> ➤ Strike up a conversation with a stranger.
> ➤ Read, listen to tapes, blogs or watch educational / instructional videos.

LESSON 12: BUY THEM A PRESENT

If a Sifu say they never get hit, don't believe them.
The more you try, the more you get hit.
When someone hits you, don't get mad.
Instead, you better thank them.
They are your best teachers.
Not the ones that sweet talk you and tell you how great you are.
The people that point out your mistakes
are the ones who help you the most.
You better buy them a present

Ken Blanchard, author of many books on management, said, "Feedback is the breakfast of champions". Unfortunately, most people skip this breakfast. Most people avoid feedback like the plague. People on a path of mastery know that the only way they can achieve success is through constant feedback.

How you *respond* to feedback, however, can determine how willing others are to provide it. Asking for it is great, but be honest — how do you respond when someone gives you feedback? Do you debate it? Argue? Discount it? Take it in but don't change?

Here are a few tips for receiving feedback in a way that will ensure others are more willing to continue to provide it:

1. Thank the person for taking the time to provide you with input. Sounds simple, but most people don't do it. In training sessions I'll often ask people by a show of hands how many people need feedback to improve. Not surprising, everyone raises their hands. Next, I ask how many people like giving feedback. Nervous laughter and then only a couple hands. Why? Giving feedback is difficult. "What if they get mad at me? What if they quit?" If someone gets up enough gumption to give you feedback you should act like they just donated one of their kidneys to you. Okay, maybe not a kidney — part of their liver. Sincerely thank them for providing you feedback. "Hey, I really want to thank you for giving me that feedback. I know it can be difficult to do. It really helps me to improve and I consider your feedback a gift. Thank you!"

2. Actually apply it! I know, I know. Sounds obvious, but how many times have you given someone feedback and they made absolutely zero change? How likely are you to give them feedback the next time they ask? Highly unlikely. Now, you not only have to apply it, but you need to make sure other people notice you have applied it. It's easy for others to "play old tapes" and not be looking for a change in behavior even though there actually is one. We look for what we want to see. You need to get people to look for what you want them to see.

3. Make it easy — ask someone, "What should I do more of? Less of? Keep doing? Stop doing?" Even if they don't know you they can provide what Executive Coach Marshall Goldsmith calls feedforward. "If I want to be better at _____, what are two things you'd suggest I do?" They don't have to know you, only have an idea about the topic.

LESSON 13: USE YOUR IMAGINATION

There is a saying in Wing Chun:
Legs like a mountain, body like bean curd, head like a crystal.
Train your legs to sink.
Like seaweed, stick to the ground, nothing can move you.
Your body is relaxed, like seaweed flowing in the water.
Your mind is clear.
Visualize what you are doing.
Use your imagination.

There was an Air Force Captain who was a Vietnam prisoner of war for six and a half years. As you might imagine, he was in terrible shape after being held captive in horrible conditions for so long. He was so malnourished that his bones stuck through his sagging and sore-ridden skin. After his rescue, he was flown back to the US where he was going to Balboa Naval hospital in San Diego to be treated. On his way there he asked if he could stop and play golf.

The officers who were riding with him thought it was an odd request as they couldn't see how the guy was even walking, but they figured what the heck. The guy was a POW for so long might as well give him what he wants. So they got him some golf shoes, clubs, balls, and tees and let him play.

The guy goes out and plays 18 holes and shoots par! The guys with him were astonished. The POW wasn't at all surprised. He said, "I've been playing a perfect round of golf on this course every day for six and a half years."

➤ Put a candle at the level of your third eye (between your eyes and just above the bridge of your nose) when you practice Siu Nim Tao. In the first section, focus on bringing the flame towards you as you bring your Wu Sao hand back. Count slowly — one thousand one, one thousand two… all the way up to one thousand ten. Then, use the same slow count as you extend your fook sao, imagining the flame being pushed away from you. Take your time on the form — it may take you 10 – 15 minutes to do one form.

"I am enough of an artist to draw freely upon my imagination. Imagination is more important than knowledge. Knowledge is limited. Imagination encircles the world."

Albert Einstein

LESSON 14: DON'T CHASE, DON'T BE GREEDY — KEEP TO YOUR CENTER

You have to understand your center.
You have to go back there.
Move from there.
Live from there.
Don't chase, and don't be greedy.
Keep to your center.
Your center is not just physical.
You have to understand what it means for your life.

➤ Train Siu Nim Tao every day. Once on both legs and then once each side, balancing on your right and then your left leg. Work up to where you can raise your leg to the level of your solar plexus. Amongst other benefits, this will help you not to overextend since you can't while keeping your balance.

➤ Train on the Mook Jang. Because the wooden dummy never moves, it will help you stay in the correct position. Use your imagination as you perform the movements. This will help you maintain the correct position when executing movements with a live training partner.

➤ Train your other empty hand, pole and butterfly sword forms. These, too, will help you maintain proper position and help keep you from overextending.

➤ The equivalent to a form in your life is your values. Your values are those emotions which are the most important to you in your life. Notice I said emotions, and not things. The difference is important. Things (money, titles, relationships, possessions, degrees even belts in martial arts) are means to an end (security, love, success, making a difference, achievement, growing). Many people search greedily after a means and don't understand why it doesn't bring them lasting peace or happiness. They end up going from job to job to job, or relationship to relationship to relationship, or achievement to achievement to achievement, wondering why none of it fulfills them. The reason is that those things are simply means to more important ends. Once you understand your ends (or end values) you won't chase. Rather, you will stay centered and focused on those core values and only do things which are in line with and consistent with those core values (similar to keeping to the center line and not chasing hands).

> What are your core values, those emotions which are central to who you are as a person? Core values include: Love, Growing, Happiness, Gratitude, Joy, Fun, Passion, Security, Contribution, Variety, Vibrancy, Power, Connection, Significance, Achievement, Success, and Peace. List your top values in your journal.

> In your journal, for each of your values, give yourself a rating on a scale of 1 – 10 on the extent to which you are living by your values. If some of your ratings are lower than you would like, say a 6 out of 10, what would it take to get to a level 8? To a level 9 or 10?

LESSON 15: STAY WITH WHAT COMES

There is a saying in Wing Chun:
Stay with what comes,
Follow as it retreats,
Thrust forward as the hand is freed.
Don't do before, don't do after, you must move at the same time.
To accomplish this, you can't be ahead, you can't be behind.
Don't think about what happened before.
Don't try to predict what will happen next.
Connect, just let it happen.
Then respond, don't react.

Practice a lot of single and double hand chi-sao. Start slowly and stick — stay connected. There are dozens of different drills to do. Keep at them so that you just go with what your partner gives you.

During your day, be aware of your expectations for others. Try engaging with others with no set expectations. Do your best to stay with them, being fully present. Most people find it's harder to do with the people closest to you, but aren't those the people you really care the most about?

LESSON 16: LET YOUR HEART AND MIND OPEN

Stay with someone in a conversation.
If you go too far ahead, you are not listening.
You are thinking of what you are going to say.
If you are behind, you will miss what the person is saying.
Stay with the person.
Try to be really listening, not commanding.
Let your heart open, let your mind open.
Connect with them.
Your word is my word.

For one day make a conscious effort to be totally present when you are with someone. As he or she talks, make a conscious effort not to judge. Rather, completely focus on the person and be totally present. Make eye contact. Notice his or her body language, words and tone of voice. Try letting their voice go into your ears, then cycle it down to your low diaphragm and only then speak. Notice if you feel like jumping in — resist it and practice patience. At the end of the day, notice if it was hard of difficult for you to do. If difficult, why? Then try again the next day and the next and…

When you drill in your Wing Chun practice, notice the same thing. Are you judging (your partner, or even yourself)? See if you can sense your partner's energy. Take it in (through your hand, for example), bring it down to your low diaphragm and then out again.

Be like water making its way through cracks.
Do not be assertive, but adjust to the object,
and you shall find a way around or through it.

If nothing within you stays rigid, outward things will disclose themselves.
Empty your mind, be formless, shapeless, like water.
If you put water into a cup, it becomes the cup.
You put water into a bottle and it becomes the bottle.
You put it in a teapot, it becomes the teapot.
Now, water can flow or it can crash.
Be water, my friend.

Bruce Lee

LESSON 17: ACCEPT

Don't fight it.
Accept it.
Don't cling and don't try to avoid.
Accept.
Accept doesn't mean not to act or submit.
It means don't judge: good, bad, right, wrong.
I like this. I hate this. I don't care about this.
Don't think about good or bad.
As soon as you do you are stopping your mind.
You are labeling. Make your mind flexible,
Without preconceived notions or thoughts. Be open.

As you go about your day, notice your inner dialogue. It has been said that the loudest voice we hear is our own, and that we talk to ourselves an average of 50,000 times a day. What is your inner voice saying to you? Is it encouraging you? Judging you? Criticizing you? Helping you?

When you are with someone, how often do you want to start your sentence with the word ...BUT? That's judging. That's labeling. Try the word AND instead. For example: I can see your point, and I'm wondering if there isn't another way to look at this. Or, I appreciate where you are coming from. If I were in your shoes I'd probably feel exactly the way you are and I really think we are after the same thing....

"Thinking is easy. Not thinking is hard."

Sifu Francis Fong

LESSON 18: TEACH FROM THE HEART

You have to decide why you want to teach.
It can't be for your ego.
It has to be to help other people.
I'm a teacher.
It doesn't matter whether I get paid $1,000 or nothing,
I will teach the same way.
Teaching has to come from the heart.

This lesson is really about passion — a passion to help other people, a passion strong enough to flex your style — from teaching, to coaching, to guiding — depending on what the other person needs, not necessarily what you want. In your journal jot down the answers to the following questions:

➤ What are you passionate about? What would you do even if you didn't get paid?

➤ If you are a teacher, why do you teach?

LESSON 19: PLANT SEEDS

A teacher isn't about a length of time.
Like a friend, a teacher can be with you for a long time
Or only for a moment in time.
One meeting could be it.
Either way, they are no less a teacher, no less a friend.
For most people, your job is to simply give them a seed.
A seed is potential. It's up to them to water it, nourish it, take care of it.
Give for as long as you have with them, then let them go.
Just plant seeds.

➤ Who was the best teacher / instructor / coach (manager) you ever had? What made them the best? What specific qualities did they possess? How did they impact you?

➤ What can you do to more effectively and consistently embody those characteristics in your teaching (managing) practice?

LESSON 20: LOOK BUT DON'T SEE

Look without seeing,
Hear without listening.
Look but don't get hooked.
Don't get caught up too much in one thing,
Otherwise you will over-commit.
You'll get caught.

Let me share with you a few approaches for not getting "hooked" and for focusing versus concentrating. The first is related to your Wing Chun practice and the next three are more general in nature.

➤ When drilling, make sure you sink down and relax your neck, not forward and not pulled back. Just resting in a neutral position, make sure your neck muscles and shoulders are relaxed. Focus on not moving your structure — keep your feet grounded, low diaphragm sunk down and chest muscles relaxed. Don't allow yourself to be distracted by your partner's hand. Focus on the center.

Tell a different story: When you are dealing with an issue it's easy to get caught up in your own perspective, to start believing your own story (which is always your interpretation of the situation). Discipline yourself to ask a different question. Instead of "Why is he such a jerk?", or "Why did she do that?" ask "How would he describe that story?", "How would she explain it?" or, "If I only thought the best of this person, what could be another possible explanation for their behavior?"

Future pace: When you find yourself getting hooked, try asking one of the following questions:
1. How much will this matter in 5 years?
2. How important is this in the bigger picture?
3. Is this really worth being upset over?
4. What will happen if I set this aside for a bit?

Worry list: Most people have a To-Do List. Once you write it down, then you know you will come back to it so you don't have to think about it until it is time. What would happen if you had a To-Worry List? A list of things you know you need to attend to but are not so critical that they need immediate attention. You may find that once you write it down, you can release that attachment. Later, when you revisit your list, you could find that you have a completely different feeling about and approach to the issue.

LESSON 21: COOPERATE, DON'T COMPETE

Don't compete. Cooperate.
Push each other to get better. That's the best way.
Sometimes you will be better so teach your partner.
Sometimes others will be better than you,
Hopefully they will share what they know with you.
You are better than someone else? Who cares?
They are better than you? Big deal!
Just try to help everybody, that's the most important thing.

Being overly focused on competing, especially when training, stems primarily from one of three reasons: being concerned solely or primarily about yourself, being afraid of losing (or not being good enough), or believing that winning is more important than developing.

1. Being concerned solely or primarily about yourself — if this describes you (at least at times), you are most likely asking yourself "How am I doing?" Instead, ask yourself, "How are my partner and I doing? How are we helping each other to get better? What did I do to make sure my partner improved?" Radical suggestion — actually ask your training partner (business partner, spouse…) How was this session for you? How was I as a training partner? What did I do that you liked? Didn't like? What can I do in the future to help you learn more effectively?

2. Being afraid of losing (or not being good enough) — if this describes you (at least at times), you most likely have a rule (or rules) for what has to happen for you to feel good about an outcome. Discover your rules directly — How do you feel when you (get hit? Make a mistake?) What does making a mistake / getting hit mean to you?

3. Believing that winning is more important than developing — remember, we're not talking about competition or a self-defense situation here. We're talking about training. So, if you only put yourself in situations where you win, how likely is it that you will improve? What would be a better rule?

LESSON 22: LITTLE BY LITTLE, ALMOST THERE

In teaching, don't show them something they can't see.
Don't ask them to feel something they can't feel.
Stay at their level, move the target little by little.
Let them know they are almost there but not quite.
That way they believe they can do it.
Then they keep trying, they keep improving.
In the same way, you have to believe for anything to work.
If you don't believe, it will never work.

You may be familiar with the story of Roger Bannister, now Sir Roger Bannister, MD. On May 6, 1954, the then medical student and physiologist became the first person to run a mile in under four minutes. Up until that point, medical doctors, physiologists and coaches all concluded that it was physically impossible to run a mile that fast. But on that day at Iffley Road in Oxford, England, Roger ran a mile in 3 minutes 59.4 seconds.

From a physical standpoint, he had a strict training regimen which included a barrage of physiological tests. From a mindset perspective, he accomplished this feat using two approaches. One was the power of visualization. Every time he ran he put a little slip of paper into his running shoe with the time 3:59 to remind him of his goal. The second approach was breaking down a big goal into micro-goals. He looked to shave off fractions of a second, little by little getting to his goal.

What Roger Bannister did was certainly impressive. What happened after he broke the record, at least in terms of the power of belief, is even more so. Remember that until he broke the four minute mile no one in history had ever done so. Yet, within a year of him setting that record, 37 other runners did the same thing. Within two years, over 300 runners ran a mile in under four minutes.

Why? Did they suddenly become better and faster? Yes and no. What happened was the mental barrier of a 4 minute mile was dashed, which allowed their physical potential to become realized more fully.

How can you use this? For you to believe something, you either have:

1. Personal experience (or references)
2. Second hand references (things you read, heard about, saw)
3. Imagined references

Which are the most powerful? Did Roger Bannister have any personal experience of running a mile in under 4 minutes until he did it? No. Did he have any second hand references? No. What did he have? Only his imagination that it was possible.

The most powerful combination is to use all three approaches:

Personal References:
➤ What have I done in the past that is like this?
➤ What am I good at that will help me here?

Second-Hand References:
➤ Who has done this before who can help me?
➤ How have other people done this?
➤ Immerse yourself by watching videos, getting coached, mentored, etc.

Imaged References:
➤ Practice visualizing — it is best if you do it first thing upon awakening and right before you go to bed
➤ Create a vision board of brilliant, vivid images related to your goal
➤ Create Micro-Goals. The Navy Seals have the Big Four of Mental Toughness:

1. Positive Self-Talk
2. Visualization
3. Arousal Control (using breath control to mitigate over-stimulation)

4. Micro-goals

Micro-goals are small steps along the way (little by little). If the goal seems too far away and unreachable, it is easy to give up. If instead you focus on the next little step (one more push-up, one more second holding your leg up, completing one more repetition), then it seems much more achievable and those little steps add up to the bigger goal.

"I have yet to find a man, however exalted his station, who did not do better work and put forth greater effort under a spirit of approval than under a spirit of criticism."

Charles M. Schwab, first president of the U.S. Steel Corporation

LESSON 23: YOU ARE YOUR BEST TEACHER

You might be with your teacher for an hour or two a day
But you are with yourself twenty-four hours a day.
You are your best teacher.
A teacher can teach
But you are taught only when you make it part of yourself.
You have to make it your own.
Trust yourself and your own nature.
You must believe in yourself.

How do you learn? Do you have to see it? Do you remember things best if you hear it? Do you have to feel it?

➤ Some people are **Visual Learners**, meaning they learn best by seeing things. In fact, if visual learners can't get a good picture of what it is they are trying to do, they struggle to embed an idea, movement, technique or concept.

➤ Some people learn best if they hear things because they are **Auditory Learners**. When teaching, I often instruct people to break a movement down by counting out loud. It's interesting when people break it down and count out loud, many do much better than simply trying to perform the movement silently.

➤ Others are **Kinesthetic Learners**, meaning they have to feel a movement. Once they feel it, they can grasp the idea very quickly.

➤ Many people learn best by **teaching** because it forces them to break things down and explain it to others.

Understand how you learn but also realize that others may learn differently. If you are a teacher, make sure you use multiple teaching approaches to ensure that students with different styles are able to learn.

"A teacher for a day is like a parent for a lifetime."
Chinese proverb

LESSON 24: VISUALIZE WHERE YOU WANT TO GO

When you train your mind
then your body will come along.
When your mind knows what to do,
your body doesn't have to work so hard.
You know people say, "No Sweat"? Why?
Because it's easy, they don't worry.
Train your mind first,
visualize what you want.

The power of visualization is amazing. Your subconscious can't differentiate between an actual experience and something that is imagined. Neither can your body to a large extent (ever wake up in a cold sweat from a dream?). However, many people don't visualize. Why? Three reasons.

1. They think that everyone else can create detailed, vivid images and theirs are not. So they don't. What they are failing to realize is that visualizing is a skill that can be developed just like anything else. Like everything else, you need to work at it. Like drawing a picture, you begin with a rough sketch. Little by little, you add more detail, more color. Train yourself to be good at it. Also, post real pictures to remind yourself of your goal.

2. They think that visualizing is limited only to what you see. While important, use other senses, too. How would you feel? What would you hear? If smell and taste come into it, use them as well. In fact, the more senses you can bring into your "visualizing", the better. Train your mind to hold a detailed sense of what you want. It will get your brain working for you due to a concept called Cognitive Dissonance, which basically means that your brain doesn't like there to be a differ-

215

ence between what you envision and what you are actually experiencing. This will motivate you to change your reality in order to line up with the image you have.

3. It takes practice. It's easier for many people to be active than to sit silently and visualize. Like anything else, though, with practice you will get better.

> *"You should sit in meditation for 20 minutes a day,*
> *unless you are too busy;*
> *then you should do it for an hour."*

> Zen saying

LESSON 25: CONTROL YOUR MIND, CONTROL YOUR BODY

You have to work on your centering.
Once you are centered,
then you can control the mind.
And when you discipline your mind,
you can control your body.
Without control of your mind and body,
you can never master yourself.

The easiest and fastest way to control your mind and your body is to control your breathing. How long can you go without food? Weeks. How about water? A few days. How long can you go without breathing? Minutes. This should give you a pretty good idea about where your focus should be.

Most adults breathe around 16 times a minute (between 12 and 20 inhales and exhales). Because of a sedentary lifestyle, many people use only their upper diaphragm and breathe in a very shallow manner so their bodies are not getting needed oxygen. If you slow your rate of breathing down and breathe more fully, you can change your brain waves and improve the oxygen saturation levels in your blood.

There are five types of brain waves: gamma, beta, alpha, theta and delta. Gamma has the highest level of brain activity, up to 100 cycles per second (CPS). The function of gamma is believed to be used for information processing functions which include attention, cognition and memory. It is also thought that gamma waves integrate and unify the various sensory inputs.

Beta (between 12 – 16 CPS) is the brain wave activity most people experience on a daily basis, and deals with concentration, problem

217

solving and survival, but it is also associated with anxiety, disharmony and anger.

Alpha (8 – 12 CPS) is the brain wave activity where we feel more relaxed, better able to learn, more adaptable, and more open to suggestion.

Theta (4 – 8 CPS) brain waves are linked to daydreaming, imagination, and inspirational thinking. You would experience this right before falling asleep, between being awake and dreaming.

Delta brain waves (3 -4 but can go as low as 1 CPS) are experienced during deep sleep, and is the brain wave activity we are primarily in during our first two years of life.

If you breathe the normal 12 – 20 breaths per minute, you will most likely stay in the beta brain wave state, where you may experience anxiety, racing thoughts and unease.

As you decrease your rate of breathing you will increase the percentage of alpha, theta and even delta brain waves. Many people report having more energy and increased cognitive ability as a result.

People who do breath work routinely reduce their rates of breathing to 4 times per minute and really experienced practitioners can get to 1 time per minute.

Like anything, you need to work on it. Here are a few different types of breathing exercises you can try:

4 Breath — Inhale deeply for 5 seconds, hold your breath for 3 seconds, exhale all the air out fully for 5 seconds, then hold 2 seconds at the bottom. Repeat this cycle 3 times to complete the full minute. This will get you to 4 complete breaths per minute. Try it for 5 minutes total.

Box Breathing — I learned this from Commander Mark Divine, former Navy Seal Commander, who teaches this in his *Unbeatable Mind* and *SealFit* programs. Inhale, hold, exhale, and hold are all the same length. You may start with 4 seconds in, expanding your low diaphragm fully, hold for 4 seconds, exhale fully for 4 seconds, and then hold again for 4 seconds. You can increase the time as you feel comfortable. Set a timer for 5 minutes.

Segmented Breathing / Breathwalk — I was introduced to this type of walking and breathing by Gurucharan Singh Khalsa when I was training in Kundalin Yoga. The Russian martial art of Systema also uses this type of breathing. First, attempt to release any tension in your body that you don't need (which for most people is at least 50%! Think of toddlers — there are very soft and relaxed but also very strong). This exercise pairs your breath with a step. As you walk, breathe in through your nose and out through your mouth. Start out by taking two breaths in as you take two steps, then exhaling twice as you take the next two steps. Build it up little by little — four steps and four inhalations, four steps and four exhalations. If you are using two steps, then you would use one breathe to fill half your lungs and the second breath to completely fill your lungs. On the exhale you would push out half the air on the first, and the remainder on the second. If you use four breaths then each inhalation / exhalation would be ¼ capacity, and so on. It might take you a bit to get the hang of segmenting your breathing. You may find that you inhale or exhale too much on the first breath, but with a little practice you will get it. See if you can work up to 10 segmented breath steps. In Kundalini Yoga, Gurucharan teaches the inhale and exhale through the nose. Try both and see which one you prefer.

"When you want to move, or want to talk,
first examine your mind.
And then, with firmness, act in a proper way.
When you feel desire or hatred in your mind,
do not act or speak, but remain like a log."

Shantideva, 14th Century Monk

"In this very breath that we take now
lies the secret that all great teachers try to tell us."

Peter Matthiessen

LESSON 26: AND 1 AND 2 AND 3...

And one and two and three.
And helps you work on the connection,
the space between the techniques.
Pay attention to the timing, to the connection.
When you practice, do so with a constant flowing
of both the physical movement and your thinking.
Don't just think about the outcome, think about the connection.
But you have to be relaxed. Don't force it.
Like nature, let your practice develop naturally, too.
Otherwise you will always be rushed.

➤ When practicing, always use **and** between counting repetitions or movements. If you feel that there is a break to that flow, physically or mentally, slow down. Keep at that pace until you can speed up with the same flowing. Slow is smooth, smooth is fast.

➤ When speaking with someone, work to have the same flow and connection. In improvisation, you are always encouraged to agree with what the person before you said, no matter how bizarre, to build on it and keep the conversation going. In real life, agreeing with the person helps you to align with either their intent or their perspective. Try this. After someone makes a point that you don't particularly agree with, work on keeping the connection with the person and say, something like, "I appreciate your perspective and if I were in your shoes I'd probably feel exactly the same way, **and** I wonder if there isn't another way to look at this issue?" OR "I appreciate your intent here, and appreciate that you are trying to _____, **and** I'm wondering if there isn't a way to _____ while still achieving _____ (the time line, the cost, etc.)?"

Zen Archer Game, by Itapua Beira Mar.

This is a body game (Jogo do Corpo in Portuguese) I was introduced to it in an Ido Portal Movement X Workshop. It is a fun, interactive process that incorporates the essential fundamentals of the Capoeira game through interacting with various body techniques. There are a number of ways to play the game but here is one. With a partner, you each take turns moving in a certain way (it could be a strike, a grab, a kick, a step, a sweep, head butt, elbow, lunge, etc.). There is to be absolutely no contact and it is to be performed very slowly by each person. The initiator performs a movement slowly with plenty of telegraphing so that the responder knows where the movement is going. The responder moves only just enough to get out of the way (this could be millimeters) and no more. As soon as the responder is out of the way, he or she initiates a movement, again slowly without contact and plenty of telegraphing. Go back and forth, trying all different types of movements. Other options:

A) Stay with one partner for one minute then switch and get a different partner;

B) One person stays the initiator for a period of time (say one minute) then switch.

C) Use poles or sticks to add another element to the movement.

➤ **Forms**. Practice your Siu Nim Tao form, counting, using **and** between every movement, focusing on the connection between the numbers.

➤ **Breath Work.** Practice your breath work using **and** between counting.

LESSON 27: WORK ON YOUR FOUNDATION

Everyone is always concerned about their hands.
If you don't have the foundation, your hands are not gonna be good.
Nobody has good hands and bad footwork.
Working only on your hands and not on your footwork is like
dressing up nice, shirt, tie, hair, everything,
then going out with no pants on.
Practice your footwork

➤ **Forms.** If you know Chum Kiu, any part of the Mook Jang or Wooden Dummy, Bil Jee, Butterfly Swords, or 6 ½ Pole forms, once a week only work on the footwork of the form, don't do any of the hand techniques.

➤ **Closed Eye Moving**. Make sure you have plenty of space and there are no hazards. Then practice your footwork with your eyes closed. Move slowly and truly feel each movement, pouring your body weight into your supporting leg before you move off it.

➤ **Closed Eye Kicking**. Try your kicks with your eyes closed. Start by doing one kick with your eyes open and the next one with your eyes closed. Build up to where you are kicking 5 – 10 reps with your eyes closed.

➤ **One Legged Standing**. Put one leg up on a table, box, chair or counter, whatever level is appropriate for you. Pull back your relaxed fists to your upper chest. Breathe deeply, and close your eyes if you can without wobbling. Time yourself on one leg then switch. Build up over time.

➤ **Tire Kicking**. Get an old, regular car sized tire. Practice your low kicks on it — pak gerk, gan gerk and so gerk. You can also practice with a partner, kicking the tire back and forth. This will surely develop your kicking power and a solid base.

➤ **Low Dummy Arm Circles**. Balancing on one leg, raise the other and extend it fully in front of the dummy. Extend your toes and make small circles around the low dummy arm. Work up to 50 at a time on one leg. Start with clockwise circles, and then go to counterclockwise circles.

➤ **Train the Long Pole**. Training the long pole will help with your footwork and transition from a low horse stance to a cat stance smoothly and quickly.

LESSON 28: LEFT SIDE, RIGHT SIDE

The left side of your brain controls the right side of your body.
The right side of your brain controls the left side of your body.
You can't only use one side — you will be off balance.

➤ **Alternate Side Focus.** When practicing, focus on the opposite side
of the technique you are working on. For example, if you are using
your left arm for bong sao, focus on your right side. If you are kicking
with your right leg, focus on your left.

➤ **U Breath (Also Called Alternate Side Breathing).** This practice
works to balance the left and right hemispheres of our brains, and is
said to help regulate body temperature. Sit comfortably with your
spine erect and shoulders relaxed. You will be using your right thumb
and index finger to gently press on your nostrils as described below.
Let your elbow relax against your chest. Close your eyes and your
mouth as you will be breathing from your nose only. Try to make your
exhales slightly longer in duration than your inhales.

➤ Press your thumb against your right nostril and breathe out gently
but fully through your left nostril. Now breathe in from your left nostril and then press the left nostril gently closed with your index finger.
Remove your right thumb from your right nostril, and breathe out
gently and fully from the right.

➤ Breathe in from your right nostril and exhale from your left. You have now completed one round. Continue inhaling and exhaling from alternate nostrils for 9 full rounds.

LESSON 29: LET ENERGY FLOW THROUGH YOU

The energy of the body and mind is very real, and very powerful.
People get so caught up in it being magic or some secret technique.
It's not but you have to work at it.
We use all kinds of energy every day.
You may not understand it but you can use it.
It does no good to talk about energy if you can't use it.
Energy can only flow through when you are open.
When your mind and body are focused and relaxed.

Research done at the Menninger Clinic in Topeka, Kansas in the United States from 1983 to 1995 showed that healers can generate bio-electricity1. Connected to a voltmeter these healers were able to generate electrical surges ranging from 4 to 190 volts, lasting for a period of 0.5 seconds to 12.5 seconds. These surges are 10,000 times the voltages registered by the heart in EKG recordings and 100,000 times greater than EEG voltages recording brain wave activity.

If you've never felt it before you may have trouble believing it is real. Once you have, you know it is.

Whether or not you ever use it to heal or help someone else, developing a qigong practice has wonderful benefits for yourself. There are many qigong exercises you can do. One of the best is practicing your Siu Nim Tao form. Be sure you relax, visualize and breathe naturally, fully and deeply.

"Try to avoid patterns and repetition.
Mix things up and let qi flow smoothly.
Remain flexible and relaxed in all you do.
This is to truly understand qigong."

Duan Zhi Liang, Qigong Sifu and
Doctor of Traditional Chinese Medicine

LESSON 30: REPETITION

Keep practicing over and over.
People ask me, 'How can I get better?'
Simple.
Practice. That's it.
Do it over and over.
Then it gets embedded in your muscle memory,
Your nervous system.
You will just respond.

In 1991, Anders Ericsson and his colleagues at the University of Florida undertook a comprehensive study on the causes of outstanding performance. They used violinists as subjects at the renowned Music Academy of West Berlin in Germany. The students were divided into three groups based on the assessments of professors at the school and objective criteria, such as placement in open musical competition.

The first group was comprised of those considered outstanding — students who were expected to become international soloists — the highest achievement for violinists. These students were considered by many to have a musical gene.

The second group were those considered extremely talented, though not at the level of the elite performers. These students were expected to play with top orchestras around the world, but never as soloists.

The third group consisted of those deemed to have the least skill on a relative basis. They were students studying to be music teachers and their admission standards were far less rigorous by comparison.

Through detailed interviews and exhaustive analysis, the researchers found that there were essentially no widespread differences between the three groups. They all started practicing when they were about eight years old, they all decided to become musicians before they were

227

fifteen, they all had similar numbers of music teachers (around four), and they all had exposure to other instruments (most played two).

Ericsson and his team found one remarkable difference, though, which was both unexpected and significant. By the age of twenty, the students in the first group had practiced more than 10,000 hours. This amount was more than 2,000 hours more than the students in the second group and over 6,000 more than the students in the third group.

They also discovered that there were no exceptions to the rule. That is, no one in the elite group reached that level of performance without putting in those 10,000 hours and no one who put in those hours failed to reach the pinnacle of performance. They concluded that practice, not talent, is what ultimately matters, and that the difference between performers at the highest levels and everyone else is focused dedication and deliberate effort to improve their performance.

Further research by Ericson and others supports the concept of focused effort and yet dispels the magic of 10,000 hours popularized by Malcolm Gladwell in his book *Outliers*. What they found was that certain world class level practitioners had over 25,000 hours of practice, and some had far less than 10,000 hours, but it was concentrated over a very short period of time. A sustained immersion if you will.

You need to put your time into whatever you want to master. The more you immerse yourself and the more you dedicate yourself to that practice, the further along you will be.

Decide what you want and what you are willing to commit to attain it. Mastery requires full commitment and constant focus, not half-hearted interest and sporadic practice. Prior to this, discover your WHY. Why do you want to attain mastery in your chosen discipline? What does it mean to you?

If you have a big enough 'why', you will figure out the 'how'.

"If people knew how hard I had to work to gain my mastery, it wouldn't seem wonderful at all."

Michaelangelo

LESSON 31: BE A SURVIVOR

We're not playing paddy cake.
This is about survival.
Shooting while standing there at a paper target
is different than a real situation.
Same thing in fighting.
Be a survivor.
No matter what, survivors get out.

Survival is all about being aware, adaptable and capable in any given situation. Keep these tips in mind as you practice and as you go about your daily life:

Always be aware of your surroundings:

➤ Where are you? If inside, where are the exits? Are you sitting so that you can see what is going on? Sit so that you don't have your back to anyone, where you can see the exits and the room. Use reflections off glass or mirrors to notice movement. Chum Kiu trains peripheral vision. We can pick up movement in our periphery much better than movement coming towards us. Practice developing your peripheral vision.

➤ What is the terrain like? Smooth? Slippery? Icy? Uneven?

➤ If you are in a car, would you have enough room to maneuver if someone came up behind you and hit you to box you in? Can you see the rear tires of the vehicle in front of you?

➤ If in an unfamiliar city, research areas to avoid ahead of time.

Be aware of other people:

> ➤ Do people look like they are having a good time?
> ➤ Is there arguing?
> ➤ Do you have a bad feeling about someone? Trust your gut.

Be aware of options:

> ➤ What do you have that you could use as a weapon? Your belt? Shoe? Bag?
> ➤ What can you throw? What could you use as a distraction?
> ➤ Where are the exits?
> ➤ How freely can you move?

Practice realistically. Add an element of realism to your training:

> ➤ Multiple attackers
> ➤ Weapons
> ➤ Fighting after running / climbing

LESSON 32: TRAIN HARD BUT NOT TOO HARD

You need to train hard but not too hard.
You have to understand timing,
gain sensitivity and use your imagination.
You are not going to do that if all you are doing is pounding away.

There is, in our society, the thinking that more is better. More repetitions, more weight, more difficulty; essentially doing the same things over and over again, just faster and stronger.

That is one way to train. Then you keep slamming energy drinks to keep you up in the hyper-caffeinated world. Keep doing that and let me know how it goes for you in ten years.

There is another way. Train hard — certainly, but also train smart. Build periods of relaxation into your training. That is the way of nature, of the Dao (Tao). There are 4 seasons, not just one.

Physical mastery is not just about strength. It is a complex mixture of many different variables, including strength, speed, coordination, timing, relaxation, anticipation, resilience, mobility, and more. Make sure you develop all of the attributes and not just one.

Design your training intelligently. How do you design your training? How much are you reinforcing techniques and concepts you already know versus learning new techniques and concepts? How much is high intensity physical training? Medium? Low? How much is working on mobility? Sensitivity? Reaction? Relaxation? Design

your training so that you have goals for each of the various elements:
- Strength (repetitions, weight)
- Speed
- Technical knowledge
- Endurance
- Pre-hab (an example of this is doing work on your rotator cuff muscles — Supraspinatus, Infraspinatus, Teres Minor, and Subscapularis — to avoid getting injured and having to do re-habilitation)
- Mobility
- Reaction
- Sensitivity
- Agility
- Will / spirit

Get adequate sleep. How much sleep do you get? I know, this sounds so basic like, "Be nice to your mother," but most people don't heed this simple advice. Short-term effects of not getting enough sleep are that you are tired and wired. To combat this many people use caffeine in the morning to get going and alcohol in the evening to chill out.

The deleterious effects of chronic sleep deprivation are significant and well documented and include higher risk of obesity, diabetes, and hormone imbalance.

The 3 Mile Island, Challenger and Exxon Valdez disasters were all due to sleep deprivation. 19 – 24 year olds are 4 times more likely to die in a fatal car accident due to sleep deprivation than due to alcohol.

You can be erasing all of your gains training by not getting adequate sleep, which is generally agreed to be 7 ½ hours per night. Pre-light bulb, the average was 10 hours a day. In the early days of light bulbs, it was 8 hours a day. Today the average is 6.

There are a number of reasons why we don't sleep: thinking that sleep is for the weak, lights, electronic devices, pro-inflammatory diet, and vitamin D3 (which is really a hormone) deficiency.

Here are a few tips:
- Try taking your resting heart rate (RHR) first thing in the morn-

ing. After a number of days you will have a pretty good idea of your average resting heart rate (ARHR). After that, check your RHR upon waking. If your RHR is more than 5 beats per minute more than your ARHR, scale back your training and get more sleep.

➤ Completely blacken your room

➤ Get rid of electronics in your bedroom

➤ Stick to the same schedule

➤ Wake up and go to bed the same time

➤ Good nutrition

➤ Cool bath

➤ Decrease stress — don't think about problems before going to sleep and do not do work e-mails. If it helps, create a To-Do list, and a To-Worry list. That way you can put things out of your mind before sleeping and deal with them at a later time. You can also ask yourself gratitude questions before going to bed — What am I most grateful for in my life right now? Who am I most grateful for? You can also practice deep breathing exercises or qigong.

LESSON 33: QUESTION EVERYTHING

Hurry always makes mistakes. Slow down. Take your time.
Don't just learn a technique.
Learn body mechanics then apply that to whatever you do.
Always ask yourself, 'What is the purpose?
Why am I doing this? When do I do this? Where do I do this?
The four W's first, then how.
Otherwise you will know the technique — the how — but you don't
know what you do, where you do, when you do, why you do.

In his book *A More Beautiful Question,* Warren Berger cites research
that shows children ask around 40,000 questions between the ages
of 2 and 5. A study in the UK estimated that the average Mum gets
390 questions a day from her 4 year old. The rate of questioning goes
down dramatically as kids enter their teens.

Questions can give us access to resources, help us challenge assump-
tions, identify issues, help us see things in new ways, get us to act,
allow us to learn, catalyze change, and motivate ourselves and others
to action.

The type of questions you ask are just as important as the number.
If you ask questions such as, "Why does this always happen to me?
How come I never get any better at this?" guess what? You'll get an
answer. It may not be one that helps you out, though.

Ask a better question and you'll get a better answer:

➤ Who do I know who can help me? — will help focus you on the
people you know who can help you.

➤ How can I achieve this and have fun in the process? — presup-
poses you will achieve it and get the added bonus of having fun.

➤ What did I learn today and how can I use it in the future? — helps you turn a failure into a learning event from which you can grow.

➤ What am I grateful for? — helps you focus on all the blessings in your life versus focusing on the things you don't have. Which person would you rather hang around with?

➤ What are the most effective ways to develop? — positions you to be on the lookout for the answers to your questions.

➤ How would another person view this? — helps you to see things from another's perspective.

➤ What types of questions will be most effective in helping you on your path of mastery? Jot them down in your journal.

LESSON 34: CONNECT, DON'T CONTROL

There is no enemy outside of yourself,
you are the enemy.
He is you, you are him.
Connect, don't control.
If you don't understand yourself,
You'll never understand anyone else.
See the real you, then you'll see others as they truly are.

It is very difficult to connect with others when we are overly focused on ourselves. Our attention is on our issues and problems; we are too caught up in our own world to notice what is going on with anyone else's.

In Wing Chun you learn to relax your body and mind so that you can connect with your partner. From that relaxation and connection, you can predict your partner's moves at a level that borders on mystical. It is quite useful in the practice of martial arts. It is even more useful in life, to have a level of connection with others that is so deep that you can almost know what is going on without speaking, an ability to read body language and sense subtle shifts and energies.

The foundation of this ability is to get out of our heads, and become present with another person, to focus on them without judgment and internal dialogue.

You can do this when you yourself are centered, when your mind is still, and you have a genuine interest in others. Using the ideas previously presented will help you in this area:

➤ Sinking
➤ Relaxation
➤ Balancing the left and right hemispheres of your brain

➤ Controlling your breathing
➤ Present listening

"Beware of no man more than yourself;
we carry our own worst enemies within us."

Charles Spurgeion

LESSON 35: YIN AND YANG

It can never be push-push or pull-pull,
forward-forward or back-back.
It is push and pull, forward and back.
Some days are good, some days bad,
Don't worry about it, that's the way it is.
You're going to have ups, you're going to have downs.
There is never only up, there is never only in.
You came from nothing; you go back to nothing.
You start from God you go back to God.
Everything will come back into balance.
Yin and Yang.
Why worry? You won't change the way things are.

In your practice, be aware of the yin / yang principle. Don't overcommit, but strive for balance at all times. Test your position and body mechanics using the yin and yang principles.

Ensure that you are training opposite muscle groups. For example, you probably do a lot of forward movements (driving, typing, texting, punching, push-ups, etc.). This can lead to shortened and tight chest and shoulder muscles, and elongated and weak (relatively) muscles of your back. In this example make sure you stretch out your upper chest and shoulders, and do exercises to strengthen your upper back and rear shoulders. Another example is to train your posterior chain (calves, hamstrings, glutes and back muscles) and not simply your quadriceps. If you aren't sure how to do this, seek out a qualified trainer to help you.

Train both sides.

If there is something you want that you aren't getting, check to see if you are giving it first. If you want more money, are you giving it (financially or in the form of value)? If you want feedback are you giving it? If you want love are you giving it? First give what it is you want.

LESSON 36: BE HUMBLE

Never underestimate your opponent.
Don't play around.
Be humble.

It's great, even necessary, to believe your way is the best. It helps build confidence when it is time to act. Never underestimate your opponent, though, and always look at their strengths and tactics.

When training, practice with people from other styles, of other sizes and shapes. See where you are vulnerable and work to shore up that exposure.

Be objective in your self-assessment. Share it with others close to you and ask for input to see how well your views align with others.

In business, you can do a 360 degree assessment where your direct reports (if you have them), your peers and your manager complete an assessment on you. You then compare it with your own self-assessment. After using these types of assessments for almost 20 years, I can vouch for their effectiveness. The times they don't work, however, is when the individual's self-assessment is much, much higher than everyone else's.

List out what you are good at — your strengths. Then list out areas you aren't so good at — your weaknesses. Check these with people who know you well and ask for their help in improving.

LESSON 37: LET YOUR SPIRIT GUIDE YOU

You can let your body direct your mind
And let your mind direct your spirit.
Or, you can let your spirit guide your mind
And let your mind lead your body.
One way leads to hell, the other to heaven.
If you let yourself be ruled by your body, you are an animal.
If you let yourself be ruled by your mind, you'll go crazy.
Better to let your heart rule you. Your heart will never mislead you.
You can be an angel or an animal.
It's up to you.

Beyond the physical, beyond the mental — strive to spend time each day connecting to your spirit. It will come through — sometimes in quiet solitude during meditation or prayer, and sometimes in the midst of a passionate endeavor where you lose yourself, where you forget about your body and time.

Be open. Listen.

Let it guide you.

LESSON 38: LET GO

The sky, sun, air, water. Everyone gets the same thing.
Nature is a gift from God.
If people don't realize this they are missing the whole thing.
We have been given everything we need.
If you are always calculating, always looking to get,
you will never open up.
Sometimes, the more people get the more they hold on.
They are afraid of losing what they have.
They get nice things and they worry — what if it gets stolen?
They aren't really happy.
It's okay to have nice things but the grasping is the problem.
You have nice things, great, enjoy them, but let them go.
Let go of what you are holding on to. Open your heart.
Sacrifice. Don't expect anything. Let go

My wife, Jessie, is a pediatric palliative care nurse. Her patients are anywhere from newborns to kids in their early twenties, many of whom have leukemia, cancer, brain tumors, or other severe health conditions. Many make it, just as many don't. When I have a bad day at work, I just think about what she does, what those families go through and realize that I don't have problems.

One of the characteristics of someone who has mastered his or her life is someone who is grateful, wherever he or she may find themselves at any point in time. Someone who looks at the blessings in his or her life and is overwhelmed by gratitude. The more grateful they are, the more that seems to come their way, in my experience. Always wanting more and never seeming to be satisfied is, to me, the definition of hell.

➤ Spend time every day reviewing what you are grateful for. Truly focus on all the blessings you have been given.

241

➤ Be thankful — express that thanks to others. You can do this verbally, or you could take a moment to write a hand-written note. You could also buy that person a gift. Take the extra time to discover what would be truly meaningful to them.

"If you don't appreciate what you have now,
You will never appreciate what you will get in the future."

Tripp Lanier

LESSON 39: FIND YOUR OWN WAY

You want to be powerful?
The real power comes from love. God is love.
Some people go to church to feel God, some people go to a temple.
Some people sing to feel God, some people paint.
Some people practice martial arts to feel God.
You have to find your own way to God, to that love.
Otherwise, you'll always be lost, you'll always be searching.

Growing up, every spring our family would spend Easter vacation with my maternal grandparents. The seven of us would pile into that brown Ford station wagon with the wood paneling and spend three days in the car getting from Rochester, NY to Cape Coral, Florida. My father did all the driving, and each year he would go to the American Automobile Association — AAA — and get a Triptik — a series of highlighted maps that would show him the quickest and most efficient way to his destination. This was long before GPS so this map was crucial for getting us to where we needed to go.

When we kids got older, we started to share the driving. When girlfriends and boyfriends started coming along, we took two cars (the station wagon and the orange Vega!). At one point I was driving the lead car (the lead car was the one with the map) and coming to a critical juncture. There was a fork in the road. Two lanes led in the correct direction and two lanes went off in the wrong direction. I glanced back in the rear view mirror to see where the tail car was. It wasn't too far behind, a couple cars at most, but I noticed that they were in the wrong lane. My eyes were glued to the rear view mirror, willing them to get over to the left. It was to no avail as I saw their car head off in the wrong direction. Back then we didn't have cell phones and there was no way to connect with each other. Our car had the triptik so they were lost without it.

I pulled off to the side of the road to wait. I put my hazard blinkers on and hoped that they would realize their mistake and turn around.

After what seemed like forever but was actually only an hour, they pulled up behind us. The driver had gotten distracted and wasn't paying attention, and went down the wrong route. Reunited, and with the tail car sticking to us like glue, we continued our journey and arrived in sunny Cape Coral safe and sound.

A Path of Mastery is a map, so to speak, with which you can embark on your journey. Even with a good map, we can get lost along the way. We can get distracted and take a wrong turn. But the map will always bring us back to the right path. It is my sincere hope that this book has provided to you a series of lessons to help guide you along the way.

Ultimately you have to decide where you want to go. I believe the outcome all of us are pursuing is to connect to that which allows us to feel love. I also believe each of us has an inner voice which reveals to us what that is. This inner voice speaks to us in whispers in the moments that give us goose bumps, in the moments which bring tears to our eyes, and in the moments that quiet our minds and expand our hearts.

> ➤ What brings you the most joy?
> ➤ What seems to be calling to your heart?
> ➤ How aligned are your answers above with what you actually do?

"Each and every master, regardless of the era or the place, heard the call and attained harmony with heaven and earth. There are many paths leading to the top of Mount Fuji, but there is only one summit — love."

Morihei Ueshiba

ABOUT SIFU FRANCIS FONG

Sifu Francis Fong has over 50 years of experience in Wing Chun Kung Fu, and is recognized as one of the top Wing Chun instructors and martial artists in the world.

In addition to actively teaching students at his academy, Sifu Fong has trained both amateur and professional fighters for competitions, appeared in movies and television, and travelled both internationally and throughout the U.S. to teach his highly regarded martial arts seminars, as well as conducting innovative business leadership and motivational seminars for major corporations.

Originally from Hong Kong, Sifu Fong began training in martial arts at the age of 12 years old. The promise of competition first attracted him to a Tae Kwon Do school, as well as Judo and WuShu. Several years into his martial arts training, his school friend Sifu Jason Lau introduced him to the art of Wing Chun Kung Fu. He was selected into a closed-door school led by Sifu Jiu Wan, a well-known instructor who had immigrated to Hong Kong from Southern China.

Sifu Jiu Wan and Yip Man (considered by many to be the father of Modern Wing Chun as well as Bruce Lee's Wing Chun instructor) studied martial arts together at the Jing Mo Guen in Foshan.

It was considered one of the most elite institutions in southern China, dedicated solely to the highest levels of martial arts training.

Yip Man left early, completing the Wing Chun system elsewhere, and was the first to teach Wing Chun in Hong Kong. Sifu Jiu Wan went on to become a teacher at the Jing Mo Guen. When the communists came to China, Sifu Jiu Wan went to Hong Kong and joined Yip Man's organization. Sifu Fong describes his early training under Sifu Jiu Wan as very traditional and old-fashioned training, with a LOT of sticky hands training (Chi Sao).

In 1973, Sifu Fong came to the U.S. from Hong Kong in search of new opportunities. He first went to college in Canada and then to Connecticut for work. On the weekends and summers he would travel down to New York City to train with his Wing Chun brother, Sifu Jason Lau, who had had come to New York a few years earlier. A few years later, in 1975, Sifu Fong moved down to Atlanta, GA and soon after established his own school teaching Wing Chun Kung Fu in 1976.

In 1980, Sifu Fong was asked by film coordinator Bobby Bass to help choreograph the fight scenes for the movie Sharkey's Machine. It was during this filming that he met up with Sifu Dan Inosanto (Bruce Lee's well-known student and successor). This led to a lifelong friendship with Sifu Dan and a sharing of their mutual respect and interest in the martial arts.

Sifu Fong says of him, "I respect him not only as a martial artist and teacher, but also for his attitude and philosophy." Sifu Dan later introduced Sifu Fong to Ajarn (Master) "Chai" Sirisute (the first native Thai instructor to offer Thai boxing in America). These associations sealed his move into exploring his material by mastering other systems.

Throughout the years, Sifu Fong's open-mindedness and desire to explore other arts led him to include Filipino Kali/Escrima, Jeet Kune Do, Muay Thai and Grappling arts, such as Brazilian Jiu-Jitsu and Shooto, alongside of the Wing Chun curriculum taught at his Academy while also hosting some of the top authorities in those arts for seminars in Atlanta.

Sifu Fong is currently the Georgia Representative for Guro Dan Inosanto with full Senior Instructor rankings in both Filipino Martial Arts, Lee Jun Fan Gung Fu and Jeet Kune Do. Additionally, Sifu is an Instructor in Muay Thai and is the Director of the Southeastern Region for the Thai Boxing Association of the U.S.A., under the direction of Ajarn Chai Sirisute.

Sifu Francis is an honorable member of the Defensive Tactics Instructor Association of the state of Georgia, and has been a certified Head Police Defensive Tactics Instructor, who has trained police officers, S.W.A.T. teams, and Fort Benning Rangers in close quarters tactics.

Due to his diverse background and experience, the U.S. Army sought his help in updating Army training manuals to include principles in the arts of Wing Chun, Muay Thai and Filipino Kali. He maintains Special Deputy Sheriff classification in the Training/Special Operations Division in the state of South Carolina.

ABOUT THE FRANCIS FONG INSTRUCTOR ASSOCIATION (FFIA)

Mission Statement and Purpose

The Francis Fong Instructor Association (FFIA) desires to promote the quality and standards of Wing Chun instruction for all students and instructors under the direction and guidance of Sifu Francis Fong. The Affiliate Development Program was designed by Sifu Fong for school owners and Private instructors who are unable to attend the Francis Fong Academy but wish to implement an organized program into their academy. The development of an Affiliate Development Program (ADP) and FFIA provides a structured path for individuals to gain the necessary skills, knowledge and professional program materials for instructor certification under Sifu Fong and to teach Wing Chun in accordance to the curriculum developed by Sifu Fong. Character traits such as loyalty, honesty and dedication factor in the admission process to maintain the high standards of Sifu Fong in order to develop one of the foremost global Associations available today. For more information, please visit:
 http://www.fonginstructor.com/

Alan Baker and Kevin Lee helped Sifu put the FFIA together. With membership comes detailed curricula for each belt level, along with detailed videos demonstrating the forms, drills and application for each level. The videos are both studio and live-action shots during classes and camps, and they provide a wonderful opportunity to review detail you would never get simply watching live. In addition, instructors can attend FFIA camps three times a year, all included in the monthly membership dues. Those camps are attended by some of the finest martial artists and people you'll ever meet. I hope you join the family and I get to meet you in person.

ABOUT THE AUTHOR

Jim Brault began training in martial arts in 1983 after a successful high school and college wrestling career. He trained in Tae Kwon Do under then US Olympic Coach Master Sang Chul Lee until 1986. He earned his first degree black belt under Master Nam Yell Ahn in 1987 and his second degree black belt under Master Sam J. Kim in 1989.

From there Jim studied Isshin-Ryu Karate, and was exposed to a number of different arts including Jeet Kune Do and Kali with Guro Dan Inosanto, and Muay Thai with Ajarn Chai Sirisute. It was at one of these seminars in 1991 that Jim met Sifu Francis Fong.

Since that time, he has studied Wing Chun Kung Fu under Sifu Fong and was accepted as an Apprentice Instructor in 1999, and as an Associate Instructor in 2003. He earned his black sash from Sifu Fong and is currently a Senior Instructor. He is also an Affiliate of the Francis Fong Instructor Association (FFIA) which requires ongoing study and training with Sifu Fong to retain FFIA affiliation and instructor credentials. He also currently trains in Brazilian Jiu Jitsu, Jeet Kune Do / Jun Fan Kung Fu, Kickboxing, Kali and Systema.

He is the author of *Lessons from the Masters: Seven Keys to Peak Performance and Inner Peace*, which features Guro Dan Inosanto and

Sifu Francis Fong, and co-author with Sifu Kevin Seaman of *The Winning Mind Set.*

Sifu Jim started Wing Chun Concepts in Rochester, New York in 1999. Wing Chun Concepts is a school dedicated to helping students learn and apply the concepts of Wing Chun for self-defense, health and life. He trains private students and teaches classes and seminars in Rochester, NY and in the UK.

ACKNOWLEDGEMENTS

I'd like to thank the following people who have helped contribute to this book through their comments and feedback on early drafts: Al Zepeda, Sule Welch, Kevin Seaman, Bill Hearst, Jessie Brault, Luigi Cuellar, Rachel Foladare, Dave Brault, Katie Fischette Barry, Dan Brault, Jennifer Brault and Nannette Nocon.

To Guro Dan Inosanto and Simo Paula Inosanto for the introduction and use of photos,

To Simo Tracey Fong for her reviewing of the manuscript and providing photos,

To Anya Fasolyak for her graphic design throughout the book,

To Kevin Lee for the book cover designs,

To Abbie Saunders for her work editing,

To my students for their dedication to learning Wing Chun,

And to Sifu Fong for literally changing my life.

"Study anyone who's great, and you will find that they apprenticed to a master, or several masters. Therefore, if you want to achieve greatness, renown and superlative success, you must apprentice to a master."

Robert Allen

BIBLIOGRAPHY

Healing and the Mind, by Bill D. Moyers. Doubleday, New York, New York, 1993.

The Way of Qigong: The Art and Science of Chinese Energy Healing, by Kenneth S. Cohen. Random House Publishing Group, a Ballantine Book, New York, 1997.

Frames of Mind: The Theory of Multiple Intelligences, by Howard Gardner. Basic Books, New York, 1983.

A More Beautiful Question, by Warren Berger. Copyright 2014 by Warren Berger, Bloomsbury USA, New York.

Lesson 29: 1 Elmer E. Green, Ph.D., Peter A. Parks, M.S., Paul M. Guyer, B.S., Steve L. Fahrion, Ph.D., and Lolafaye Coyne, Ph.D., "Anomalous Electrostatic Phenomena in Exceptional Subjects," Subtle Energies 2:3 (1991) pp. 69-94, and "Gender Differences in a Magnetic Field," Subtle Energies 3:2 (1992) pp. 65 – 103.

https://www.facebook.com/wingchunconcepts

https://www.APathOfMastery.com